DE
SIGN
PLAY
AN
ARRAY
OF QUIRKY
DESIGN

DESIGN●PLAY

First published and distributed by
viction:workshop ltd.

viction:ary™

Unit C, 7th Floor, Seabright Plaza, 9-23 Shell Street,
North Point, Hong Kong
URL: www.victionary.com
Email: we@victionary.com

Edited and produced by viction:workshop ltd.

Concepts & art direction by Victor Cheung
Book design by viction:workshop ltd.
Preface by Shirley Surya
Title typeface 'Ideoma SPRAY' by www.ideoma.pt

ISBN 978-988-17327-3-6

Printed and bound in China

CONTENTS

P.004
PREFACE

[1] Quoted from an interview by "Metropolis" magazine (http://www.metropolismag.com/story/20090218/marcel-wanders).

[2] Same source as the above.

[3] A term coined by Johan Huizinga in his book "Homo Ludens: A Study of the Play Element in Culture."

PLAY
TO AMUSE:
SPICE
UP LIFE
WITH IDEAS

They're everywhere now – in museum stores or quirky interior boutiques – beckoning your touch and enkindling a smile. They're so well-designed to amuse, they make heart-warming gifts than practical essentials. For those who submit to design's problem-solving mandate to concretely improve everyday living, such playful designs may not be up their alley. They may think declarations like "I am designer of the new age. I am a dreamer. I am a jester,"[1] by well-known Dutch product design maven Marcel Wanders a joke, and his frequent "Function is highly overrated"[2] comment unrealistic. These seemingly fantastical and non-utilitarian designs have nevertheless pervaded the market – a movement so evident, it seeded the idea for this book. The featured works proved not only how far and wide this play on the user-viewer has manifested in design, but also how in the eyes and minds of creatives, play is so much more multilayered in its meaning, method and effect.

The idea of "play" smacks of trivial pleasures, bordering on uselessness. Some of the works here certainly bear these marks through imaginative pretence. What can one do with ATYPYK's Polaroid photo-looking mirror (P.113) that only reflects a warped image, or Azumi and David (A'N'D)'s Cool Shade Tapes (P.124) made of adhesive tapes printed with images of shades? But these "completely unnecessary things" are what designers like ATYPYK professes to enjoy making for thrilled fans whose testimonials include "please send as much of your ideas to make people smile" and "had a great laugh just viewing them" – fulfilling ATYPYK's promises to let their users "Never Get Bored Anymore", "Find Happiness", and more. So trivial as they seem, while teasing our normative perceptions, they're no less meaningful as they resonate with people. Humans generally don't just pursue tasks and solve problems. They wonder, love, waste time, or burn their cigarettes on napkins – one of the mundane acts which Julie Krakowski explores in her Coffee and Cigarettes textile series (P.30) embroidered with marks that look like cigarette burns and food stains typically left on linens. Reflecting on the quotidian in these evocative designs is perhaps inspired by the notion of people as playful creatures or "Homo Ludens" (Man The Player), as opposed to just "Homo Sapiens" (Man The Thinker)[3]. It would be a mistake to dismiss life's trivialities based on utility. For unless there's a respect for the full range of values that make us human, the objects and technologies created are likely to be uninteresting at best, and de-humanising at worst.

Effective play arises not from high-flying design but the new spin given to familiar objects or experiences. Japanese studio nendo puts it best in their philosophy: to give people the small "!" moments that makes life interesting by reconstituting the everyday into products and scenes that people can encounter. Like the nostalgia for sharpening school pencils as you grate nendo's pencil-like chocolates (P.32) into shavings that add your dessert, or having your senses jolted with the topsy-turvy effect in seeing sofas and plants mounted against gravity on the walls of an atrium (P.192). In a world full of attention-grabbing images where we're presented with infinite choices, the intrinsic value of any thing (person, place, object) is first noted and acknowledged for how it captures our hearts and minds, how it makes us feel. The element of play has become the designers' stimulus to create products and spaces with a cult personality by engaging individuals on such visual and emotional level. From Atelier Bow-Wow's one-pattern design for the entire surface of a room in Lydmar Hotel (P.174) that disturbingly dissolves the normal figure-ground perception to Nina Mrsnik's 2D illustration on the staircase that becomes a visible 3D chair from a certain angle and distance (P.156), designers have wielded optical play to induce that "!" effect, which has also become a sensational marketing tool – for better or for worse. The bombardment of visual messages that have dulled our minds and effectively raised everyone's appetite for visual over-stimulation, seems to require such stretching of imagination and suspending of our disbelief to make us see with fresh eyes.

But whether in the format of advertising, products or installations, the intentions and effects of play can surprisingly engage us at a more cerebral way than they seem at first glance. Stolen Jewels Collection (P.42), a series of accessories using jagged extracted low-res online images of the most expensive jewellery printed and scored in leather, may come across as a teasing mimicry of computer graphics but it's Mike and Maaike Inc's attempt to play on the idea of tangible versus virtual, in relation to real and perceived value. Kumi Yamashita's wall sculpture CITY VIEW (P.198), made up of numerical blocks, is more than a stunning visual piece. With each of the blocks carefully arranged to cast a particular shadow that adds up to the illusion of a female silhouette against the balustrade, when illuminated from a single light source, it is a product of both beauty and intelligence with its ability to challenge our perception of predictable relationships between solids and their shadows. One may find Slinkachu's Little People Project (P.160) amusing, with his miniature characters photographed to contrast real life human figures in actual settings. But, beneath the humour is a call to empathise with the vulnerability of living in a big city. In many projects such as these, light-hearted elements of visual trickery surprisingly launch us to the bigger questions.

Function is also not always considered overrated in playful designs that move the heart and the mind. A double dose of surprise awaits the user-viewer of objects or spaces that trick and tickle as much as they serve your needs. Vanessa van Dam's Wristband Flyers (P.24) – wristbands fully printed with images of tattoos, sweatbands or pearls on one side and event information on the other – is such an example of how solving problems, however small but with a twist, is something innate in designers. Now that the flyer doubles up as an accessory, it will not be so easily lost. And when angle-distance optical trick is often only used to poke fun at people, Axel Peemöller's directional system (P.152) on the walls of Eureka Tower's parking lots actually makes use of this trick such that the signage can only be read if one stands (or drives) facing them in the right position. Eureka! Also, who could have imagined that stickers that look like metal rust and scratches can keep the thief off designer Dominic Wilcox's new bike for 13 days in London? It is truly an Anti-Theft Device (P.114) just through masterful visual mimicry, ultra dry wit and a playful spotlight on the banal.

Apart from a sense of humour and recreation, the notion of participation and change – the most visceral form of engagement with the user-viewer and its context – are the often-overlooked but important elements of play. us design studio Rain Positive t-shirts (P.132) whose printed messages appear only under the rain; Draft's Method of Drinking Fairytale glass (P.59) that uses refraction to complete the visual narrative of Little Red Riding Hood only when the wolf's image enlarges when water is poured in; and Jamie Wieck's transparent bag (P.58) printed with a face on one side and a pair of hands on another add up to the image of a happy owner holding the object in the bag all require the intervention of actions and surrounding elements to complete the experience of the product. How a product behaves under variable circumstances and how interfaces are devised for well-articulated product-user relationships are further displayed in POLAR's Eurocities tablecloth (P.104) on which mayors of EU cities are invited to expressively mark their opinions and drawings on, in an otherwise restrictive occasion, as well as Berber Soepboer's and Michiel Schuurman's Colouring Dress (P.122) which wearers can colour in its printed patterns to their liking.

It can be quite mystifying to fully imagine some of these highly interactive projects on print. But through the various optical and interactive means of play from which we derive the categories Angle-Distance Adapt, Blend-In Dizzy, Bounce-Off Appeal, Process-Interact, Pixel-Like and Look-Alikes, "Design•Play" seeks to reveal the communicative potentials – emotional, mental or interactive – of seemingly simplistic playful objects and spaces. We hope these quirky yet visionary works stimulate new patterns of thought and action in the visual and material culture, at the same time remind us of ourselves – sentient beings who see design as "much more than simply to assemble, to order, or even to edit," but as the words of influential American graphic designer Paul Rand ring true, "to add value and meaning, to illuminate, to simplify, to clarify, to modify, to dignify, to dramatise, to persuade, and perhaps even to amuse."

ANGLE-DISTANCE ADAPT

Take a step back. Tilt your head a little. See it? The visual revelation of these art-works in both 2D and 3D profile requires your adaptation to a certain angle or distance, nudging you to a fresh perspective.

BLEND-IN DIZZY

Figure-ground relationships are dissolved; the normal way of seeing is disturbed. With patterns seamlessly covering the surface and linear distortions taking on a ki-netic quality, get yourself to feel unsettled in a space without a beginning and an end, moving and unmoving, real and surreal.

BOUNCE-OFF APPEAL

In the context of exhibitions, prints and everyday objects, reflective surfaces have become an instrument to surprise, fool and delight viewers optically and mentally through the illusion of space and dimensions. Complete the visual narratives with a mirror that never lies.

PROCESS-INTERACT

Colour it, write on it, heat it, let it go under the rain – experience interactivity at its best as you watch the designers' creations transform in time and with your hands. These innovative forms of communication allow you to take the credit of develop-ing the desired pictorial effect.

PIXEL-LIKE

Digital tools were once used to enhance realism but with skilful 3D installations, photography, filming and production of real objects and settings, these projects present 'live' simulation of desktop environments and images we thought only exist in 'Pixel land.'

LOOK-ALIKES

Visual mimicry in everyday products, pervasive print or conceptual pieces is not mere illusions of reality. What you see is not what you get – these reproductions with their surprising functions and provocative communication trigger the emotions of some and spur the imagination of others.

BY
MEANS
'PLAY' OF

PANDORA NOTE

The black elastic cords are designed to hold the pages together while resembling the bars of the animal cages. When the notebook is in use and the elastic cord is removed, the caged-beast would be enabled to roam free.

Design: DRAFT Co., Ltd Client: D-BROS Type of Work: Notebook
Year: 2006

Process-Interact   ☞ *P.16*

EVERYTHING IN ITS RIGHT PLACE

Exhibition 'Everything in its Right Place' brings attention to dyslexia, a condition that lacks public attention at all times. The invitation focuses on the different symptoms of dyslexia with interactive graphics, encouraging users to solve the riddle of words so as to get 'Everything in its Right Place.' Typographer David Carson was one of the contributors to the exhibition.

Design: Felix Lobelius Client: Dyslexia Foundation Type of Work: Invitation
Year: 2007

Bounce-Off Appeal

☞ *P.17*

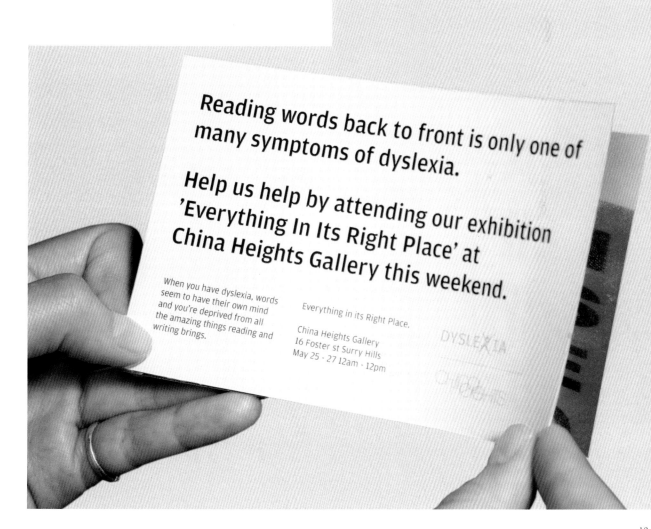

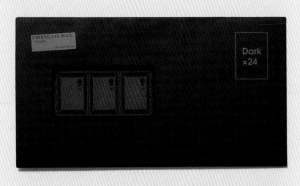

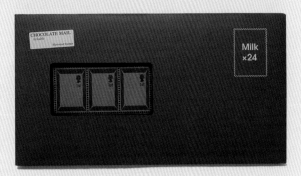

CHOCOLATE MAIL

Can you tell if they are postage stamps or chocolate slices at first sight? Thinking about how stamp designs could be improved, Ng decided to delight those who enjoy 'lick and stick' with a set of 24 1st class stamps that comes in three 'flavours' – dark, milky and white chocolate. Lick and stick, but don't eat.

Design: Toby Ng Client: Toby Ng Type of Work: Stamp Year 2008

Look-Alikes   ☛ *P.18*

WINE CARD

Koktebel wishes to greet its partners and customers with a card that represents the culture of
wine consumption in the New Year. Release the
delicate scent while you open the card and pour
the wine.

Design: Graphic design studio by Yurko Gutsulyak Client:
Koktebel Wine and Cognac Distillery Type of Work: Greeting
card Year: 2007

Process-Interact 🐦 *P.10* 🐦 *P.21*

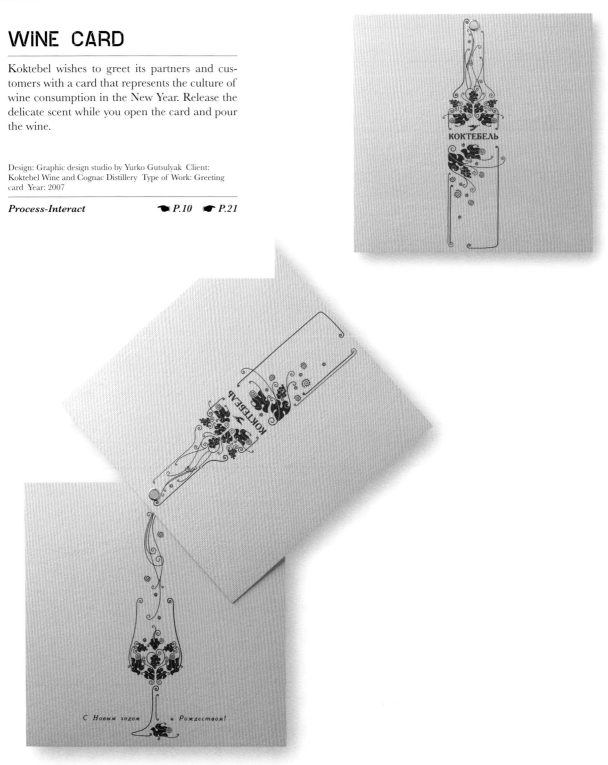

MIRROR CARD

A series of greeting cards is made from paper with a mirror surface, with illustrations drawn on both sides of the card. The narrative of each card could only be entirely revealed when the card is folded at a 90 degrees angle, projecting a three-dimensional illustration by mirror reflection.

Design: DRAFT Co., Ltd Client: D-BROS Type of Work: Greeting card
Year: 2003

Bounce-Off Appeal 🖝 *P.12* 🖝 *P.22*

melt
Milk Chocolate

INGREDIENTS: Sugar, Cocoa Butter, Cocoa Mass, Skim Milk Powder, Natural Vanilla

MADE BY MELT CHOCOLATES LLC NEW YORK, NY

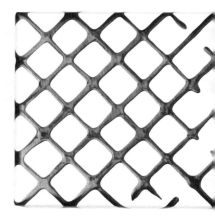

MELT CHOCOLATE

Melt, a gourmet chocolate shop, plays with the characteristics of melted chocolate with its logo and packaging with patterns that look as if they are freshly illustrated with warm, liquid chocolate. Let the chocolate speak for itself.

Design: Jesse Kirsch Client: Melt Type of Work: Packaging Year: 2008
Photography: Jesse Kirsch

Look-Alikes   🐭 *P.14*   🐭 *P.24*

WORK/PLAY POSTCARD

Postcards with black lines depicting the words 'WORK' and 'PLAY' – a real example that shows how the two things coexist without compromising each other!

Design: Melvin Galapon Client: Melvin Galapon Type of Work: Postcard Year: 2008

Angle-Distance Adapt 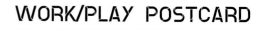 *P.62*

THE SEQUINS - THE
DEATH OF STYLE

To Ostrowski, the 'death' of 'style' is destructive, like
when the sprinkling of real sequins liberally spills out
of the shrinkwrapper when it is unwrapped. Featured
here is the album packaging of 'The Death of Style'
for the band, 'The Sequins.'

Design: Alex Ostrowski Client: Tough Love Records Type of Work: CD
Packaging Year: 2007

Process-Interact   🖝 *P.16*   🖝 *P.34*

MiRROR CARD

The Christmas card is made from paper with a mirror surface with the silhouette of bare trees, animals and a girl printed on one side of the card. The little stream and lake extends into the mirror reflection, illustrating a tranquil winter scene for the perfect white season.

Design: DRAFT Co., Ltd Client: D-BROS Type of Work: Card
Year: 2005

Bounce-Off Appeal  ☛ *P.17* ☛ *P.28*

WRISTBAND FLYERS FOR CHEMISTRY

Flyers get lost easily — so by putting this flyer around your arm, you will keep the information with you as a bracelet. The images give you the possibility to wear cuffs, tattoos, pearls or sweatbands, with details of the specific evening event printed inside the 'bracelet.' The Wristband flyers was created for party organiser, Chemistry.

Design: Vanessa van Dam, Anneke Saveur Client: Chemistry Type of Work: Flyer Year: 2000

Look-Alikes   ☛ *P.18*   ☛ *P.26*

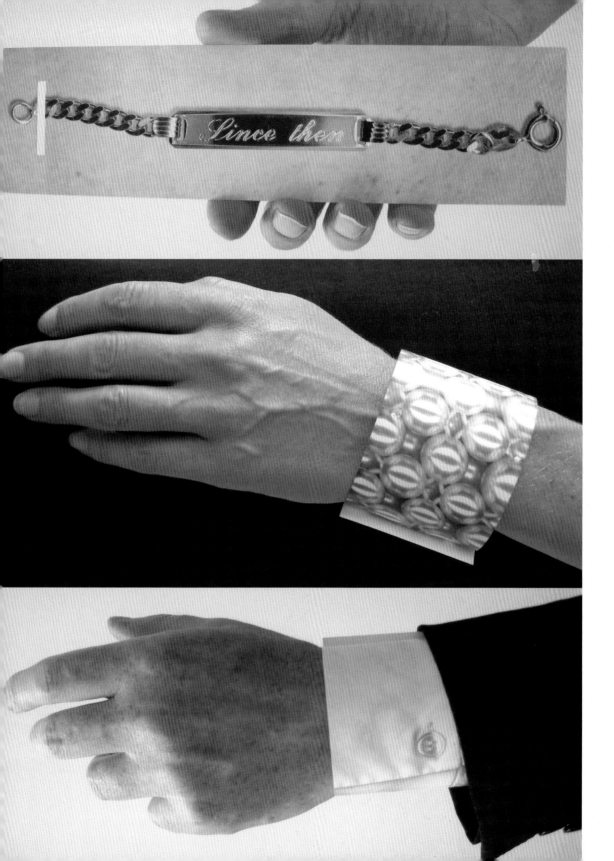

SHIRT-KERCHIEF, BLOUSE-KERCHIEF

Azumi and David (A'N'D) has new interpretations for the functions of aesthetically-pleasing kerchiefs. Featured here are the neck-kerchief-style scarfs with shirt-button front in cotton[1] and silk[2], also a ribbon-tied design with a plain front in silk[3]. Silky blouse-kerchiefs are alternatives to neck-kerchiefs with accessories, such as 'pearls[4]' and 'chains[5].'

Design: Azumi and David (A'N'D) Client: Azumi and David (A'N'D) Type of Work: Scarf Year: 2009

Look-Alikes *P.24* *P.30*

ANAMORPHIC CUPS

Anamorphic cylinders first appeared in the 1600s and became popular throughout Europe in the 18th century. Anamorphic Cups are stainless steel cups with a polished mirror finish, accompanied by porcelain saucers printed with distorted images or words. Users could only decode the hidden messages with the curved and reflective surface of the cup.

Design: K.K. Normal Client: Wings Trading (HK) Co., Ltd. Type of Work: Coffee cups Year: 2004

Bounce-Off Appeal　　🐷 *P.22*　🐷 *P.38*

COFFEE AND CIGARETTES

Work based on marks left by little accidents in everyday life, such as cigarette burns and food stains. Although the 'stains' exist as decorations, you could still find traces of the 'fault' on the fabric. It accentuates the beauty of the randomness and the ambiguity between the worn and the precious.

Design: Julie Krakowski Client: Julie Krakowski Type of Work: Embroidery, Perforation Year: 2006

Look-Alikes ☞ *P.26* ☞ *P.32*

CHOCOLATE-PENCILS

Pencil shavings are usually treated as litter, but here, they're the star! Patissier Tsujiguchi Hironobu, the mastermind behind popular dessert shops like Mont St. Claire and Le Chocolat de H in Japan, has collaborated with nendo to create these 'pencils' for a new dessert. Grate the 'pencils' that comes in varied coca blends and adorn your dessert as if it's a lovely canvas.

Design: nendo Client: Mr. Hironobu Tsujiguchi Type of Work: Product
Year: 2007

Look-Alikes　　　　　　　　　　◗ *P.30*　◗ *P.36*

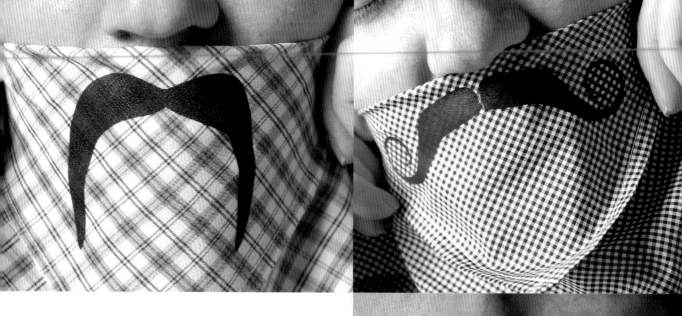

MUSTACHE HANDKERCHIEF

Next time when you get sniffles, dress your upper lip with a Mustache Handkerchief. Printed with four classic moustaches, including the handlebar moustache, and others wore by Salvador Dalí, Tom Selleck, Rollie Fingers, these hankies are available in a variety of fabrics and patterns. 100% cotton and 100% handsome!

Design: Avril Loreti Client: Avril Loreti Type of Work: Handkerchief Year: 2007-present

Process-Interact

🖙 *P.21*   🖙 *P.52*

D&AD ASDA LUNCHBOXES

Want to optimise your one-hour lunch for an escape? Get transferred to somewhere special with a set of lunchboxes that cover three distinctive scenes – 'Satisfying' (table setting with a wine glass), 'Healthy' (summer picnic setting) and 'Children's' (with toy tools in a sandpit). This project has been awarded D&AD Yellow Pencil for Packaging Design (Silver).

Design: Emma Smart Client: D&AD Student Award 2006 Type of Work: Packaging Year: 2006

Look-Alikes ☛ *P.32* ☛ *P.44*

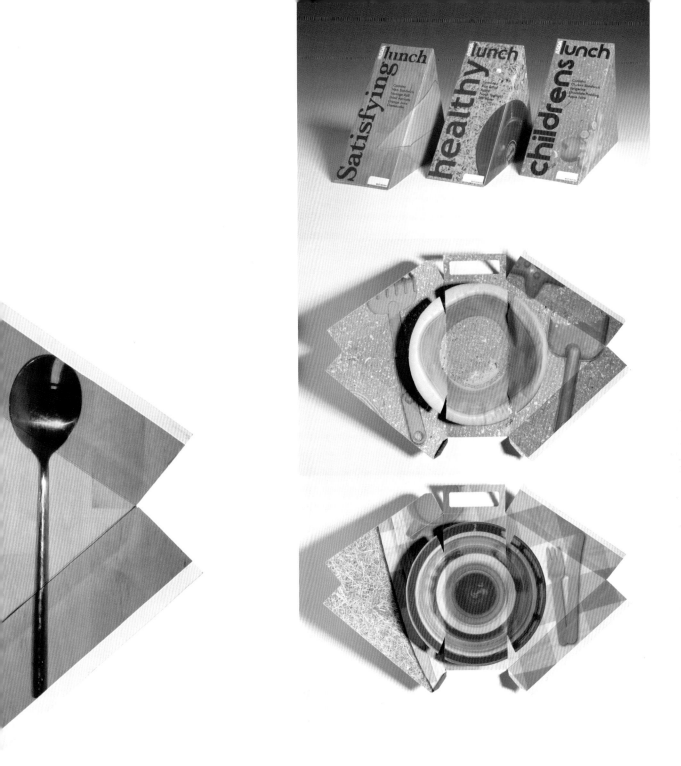

D-BROS CUP SETS

The sets of cup with a mirror surface and saucer printed with colour binding patterns in From Dawn Till Dusk[1] and vivid harlequin designs in Waltz[2] play with the age-old anamorphic effect in a pure graphical way. The design of cup and saucer turns off once the cup is placed on the saucer.

Design: DRAFT Co., Ltd Client: D-BROS Type of Work: Cup, Saucer Year: 2004-08[1], 2005[2]

Bounce-Off Appeal   *P.28*   *P.134*

2

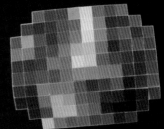

STOLEN JEWELS
COLLECTION

The collection is a new incarnation of some of the most expensive and often famous jewellery from around the world. While having the expense and intricacy of jewels stripped away and rendered as enlarged pixel squares, their essence and visual intensity are extracted. Stolen Jewels is a series of printed and scored leather accessories.

Design: Mike and Maaike Inc. Client: Mike and Maaike Inc. Type of Work: Jewelry Year: 2008

Pixel-Like

 P.136

CHARACTER MARKS

In an age where people strive to wipe clean the tell-tale imperfections on their faces, Character Marks reverses the mentality. Marks, spots, scars and wrinkling on our skin somehow define characters, for example the wrinkles formed by habitual expressions and scars caused by accidents. These adhesive patches help to acquire these features without going through ages and pain.

Design: Sarah Napier, Bethany Koby Client: Fabrica Type of Work: Conceptual Year: 2005

Look-Alikes   🖤 *P.36*   🖤 *P.46*

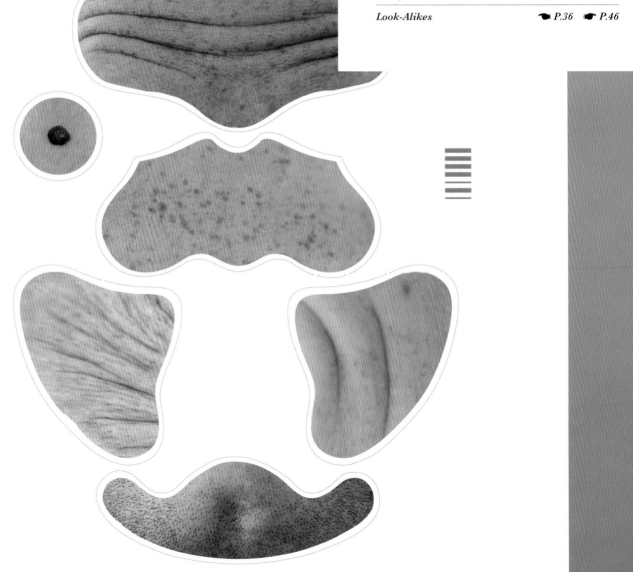

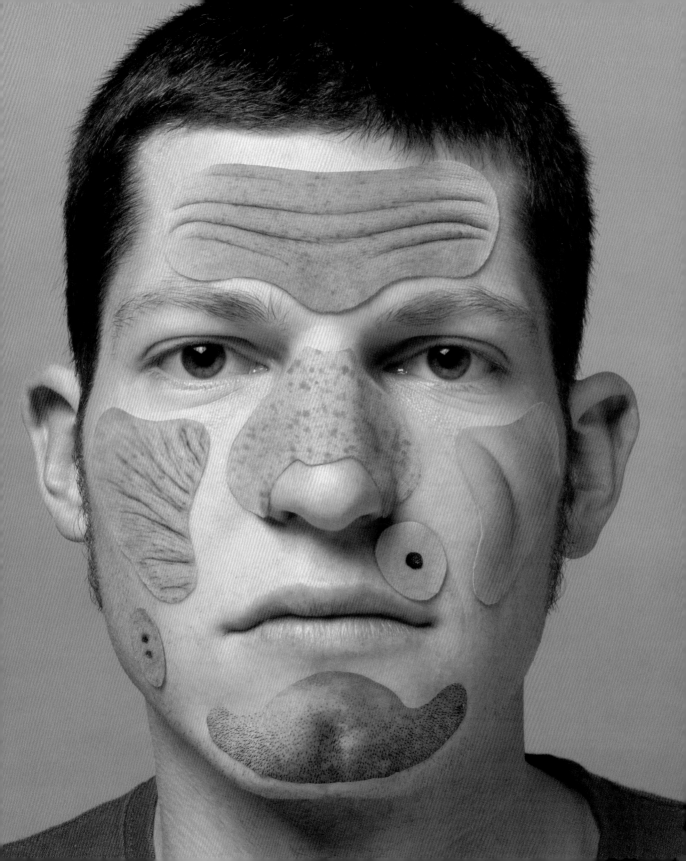

NiPPLE BADGES

The nipple badge range was originally designed to raise money and awareness for Breast Cancer Care. Nipples vary in size, shape and colour – yet we rarely talk about them or see how others' look like. The range is a fun and humourous way of conveying a serious message. It has been employed/covered by different media, including English rock band The Rolling Stones, Channel 4 and Barbican Centre, a performing arts centre in UK.

Design: Pia Knight Client: Pia Knight Type of Work: Badge Year: 2003

Look-Alikes   ☛ *P.44*   ☛ *P.48*

The *Nipple* Badges

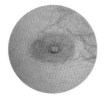
raspberry ripple

french vanilla

cream puff

ginger nut

chocolate tart

strawberry shortcake

sticky toffee pie

cookie & cream

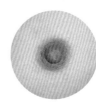
cherry pie

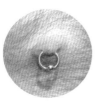
vanilla ice

strawberry & cream

fudge brownie

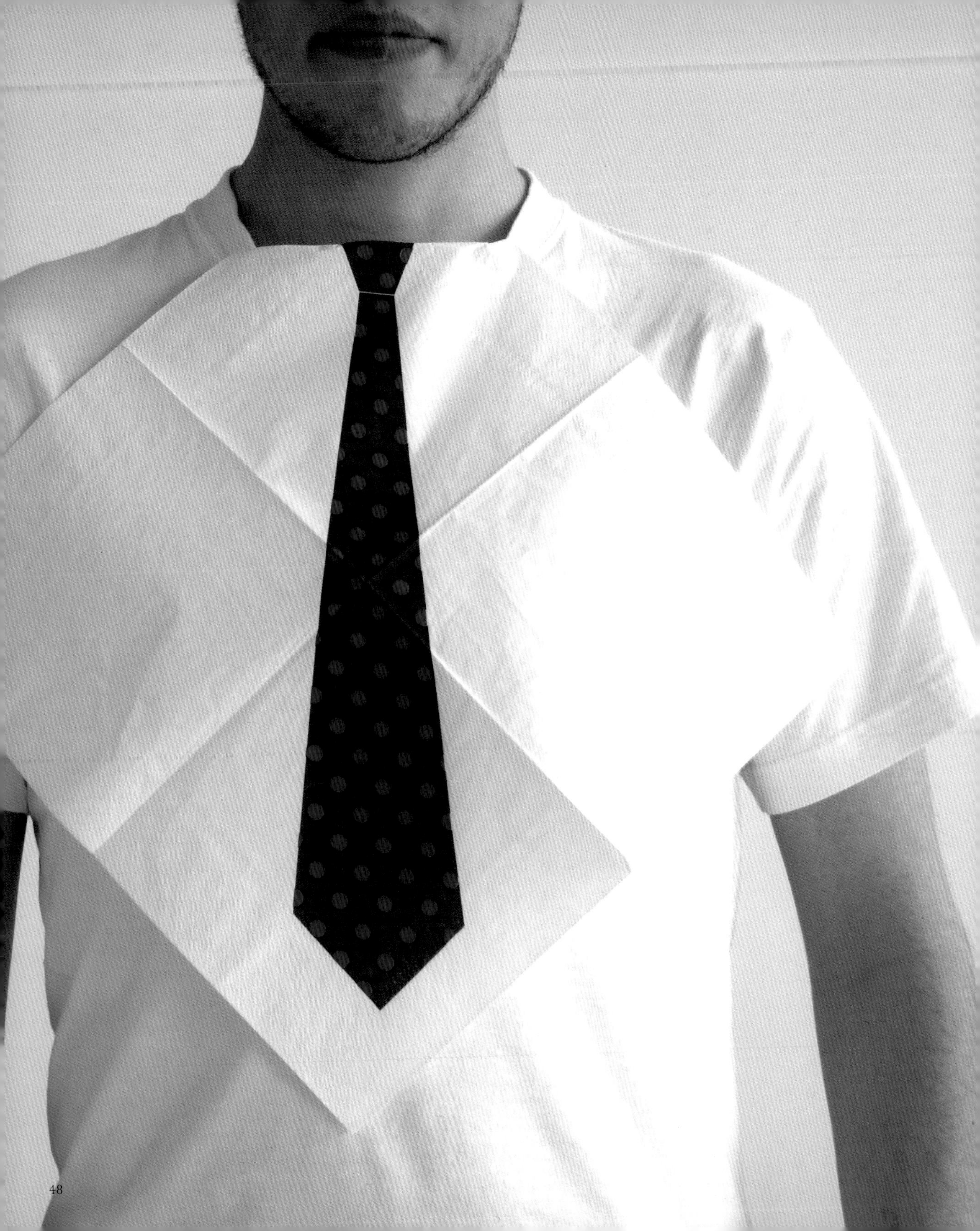

DRESS FOR DINNER

Neckties might be a bit too formal for causal dinners, but this one should be simple and easy enough to wear. Dress for Dinner is a small but fun intervention of an everyday object based on a familiar situation.

Design: Héctor Serrano Studio Client: Worldwide Type of Work: Product Year: 2008

Look-Alikes　　🐾 *P.46*　🐾 *P.50*

TALE TAIL

The notebooks are attached with a thread bookmark that looks like a horse tail. The bookmark comes in two colours. A horse illustration is printed on an inside page in connection to the idea.

Design: DRAFT Co., Ltd Client: D-BROS Type of Work: Notebook Year: 2006

Look-Alikes ☛ *P.48*   ☛ *P.51*

HANDS NOTE

The hand printed on the notebook cover is a functional yet humourous design. It 'helps' to hold the elastic band which is attached to tie the notes.

Design: DRAFT Co., Ltd Client: D-BROS Type of Work: Notebook
Year: 2001

Look-Alikes 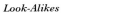 *P.50*   *P.53*

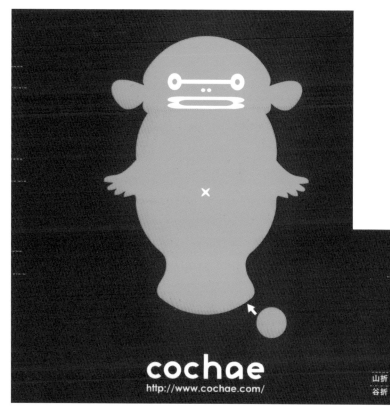

TRICK FLYER

A flyer made for cochae's own exhibition. The green monster ends up as a round circle when it is folded up like concertinas.

Design: cochae Client: KAORI NO MORI (KURIHARA CORPORATION) Type of Work: Flyer, Origami Year: 2007

Process-Interact 🐦 *P.34* 🐦 *P.54*

YEAR OF THE DOG

To a dog's home, the Chinese Year of the Dog is just too good to miss. The diary presents the tale of Chinese animal years and shaggy dog stories about the notable and notorious. The page mark becomes the tail of the dog on the cover.

Design: The Chase Typography: Stuart Price, Chris Jeffreys Client: Manchester Dogs' Home Type of Work: Diary Year: 2006

Look-Alikes   ● *P.51* ● *P.88*

BIOGRAPHY OF
MEI LANFANG

The author has already given the great Beijing opera artist, Mei Lanfang, a life back with his pen and words, and now Jingren Art and Design Studio let Mei stand in front of the readers and switch between the two important aspects of his life – on the stage and back to his normal life. Accurate calculations, precisive printing and binding are significant for the flawless result.

Design: Jingren Art and Design Studio Client: China Youth Press Type of Work: Book Year: 2002

Process-Interact ☞ *P.52* ☞ *P.56*

LETTER'S VIGNETTE

Sets of frottage cards are embossed with illustrations with various motifs. Vignettes could be made to create personalised letterheads by colouring a piece of thin paper over the raised figures. DRAFT was responsible for the illustrations and packaging designs.

Design: DRAFT Co., Ltd Client: D-BROS Type of Work: Stationary
Year: 2008

Process-Interact   *P.54*   *P.58*

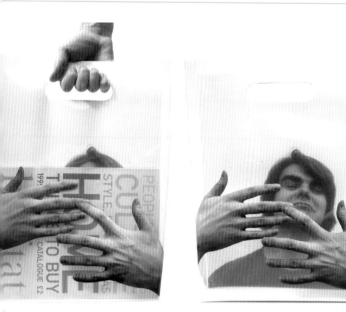

CARRIER BAGS

Wieck draws inspirations from the transparent bag he used to collect rubbish and creates the set of two carrier bags to 'carry' your shopping literally.

Design: Jamie Wieck Client: Jamie Wieck Type of Work: Carrier bags
Year: 2006

Process-Interact   🖝 *P.56*   🖝 *P.59*

METHOD OF DRINKING
FAIRY TALE

The glasses are printed with characters and scenes of some famous fairy tales, such as the Little Red Riding Hood. Changes happen when water is poured into the glass creating the lenticular effect. The vicious wolf would grow so big and strong that makes the little girl seem incapable of warding it off.

Design: DRAFT Co., Ltd Client: D-BROS Type of Work: Glass
Year: 2005

Process-Interact   ● *P.58*   ● *P.64*

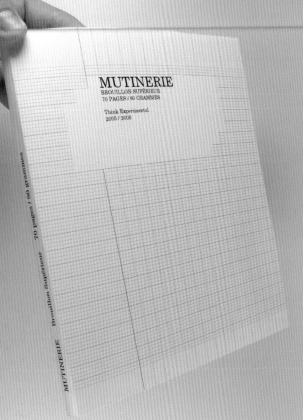

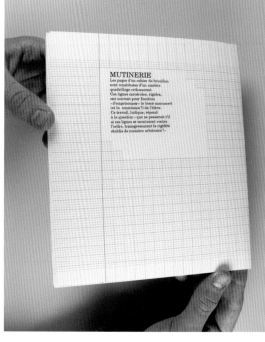

MUTINERIE (MUTINY)

Student's handwritings are often confined to the straight and rigid lines printed on the notebook pages, while Mutinerie questions the traditional notebook forms and lets its cross-ruling rebelled against the straight ones. It's never easy to write legible notes during lectures – now Mutinerie has made it even harder if you try to follow the lines.

Design: Merci Bernard Client: Merci Bernard Type of Work: Notebook
Year: 2006

Blend-In Dizzy   *P.66*

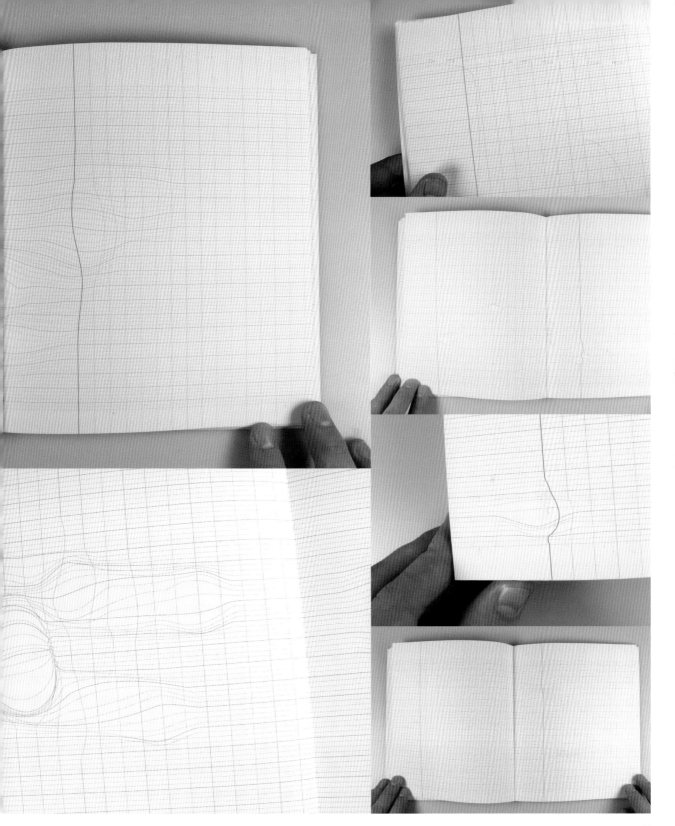

TYPE ADDICTED

Type Addicted starts playfully with its cover in an illusionary approach to explore the intriguing relationship between graphics and types. By transforming the types of the book title into some technically distorted triangular graphic elements, the book cover demonstrates straightforwardly how types can be applied into graphics and become another inspirational typeface.

Design: viction:workshop ltd. Client: viction:ary Type of Work: Publication Year: 2007

Angle-Distance Adapt   ☛ *P.20*   ☛ *P.72*

TYPE IS ONE OF THE GRAPHIC ELEMENTS THAT DESIGNERS ALWAYS GET ADDICTED TO PLAY WITH.

MOVEMENT ANATOMY

The flipbook that features the anatomy of four facial expressions – chewing, laughing, yawning and sneezing. When the pages flip over, still pictures will be transformed into real actions. The booklet is a promotional piece commissioned by a film production company.

Design: Malin Holmström Client: Movement Production Type of Work: Flipbook Year: 2008

Process-Interact   🖜 *P.59*   🖝 *P.68*

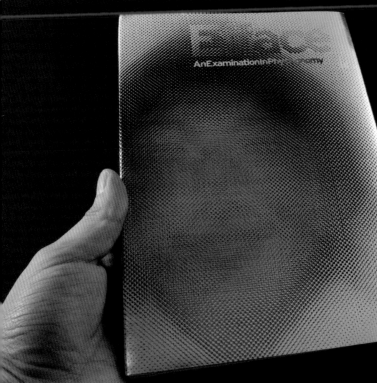

EFFACE: PHYSIOGNOMY

Human faces are infinitely complex and the recognition of facial expressions and features occupies both the instinctual and the systematic. Physiognomy analyses the face as a potential indicator of characters with 14 faces, constructed, de-constructed and fused to assemble facial appearances that readers might never encounter before.

Design: ADearFriend™ Client: Rhode Island School of Design Type of Work: Book Year: 2008

Blend-In Dizzy

🠶 *P.60*　🠶 *P.137*

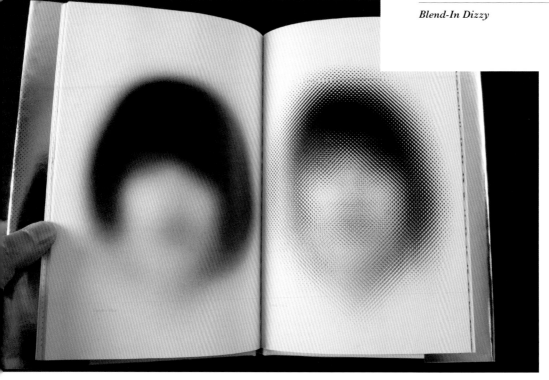

BINDI FACE, REFLECTOR FACE

Some say bindis help to retain energy and wisdom by placing it on the forehead, while some add jewels to make it a fancy accessory. FACE has created a series of bindis that comes in a range of forms, colours, shapes, and materials like fabrics, hair and other decorative elements, such as chains[1]. Some possess distinctive features such as the Reflector FACE[2], which shines in the dark.

Design: FACE Client: FACE Type of Work: Sculptural product
Year: 2008

Process-Interact   ☞ *P.64*   ☞ *P.74*

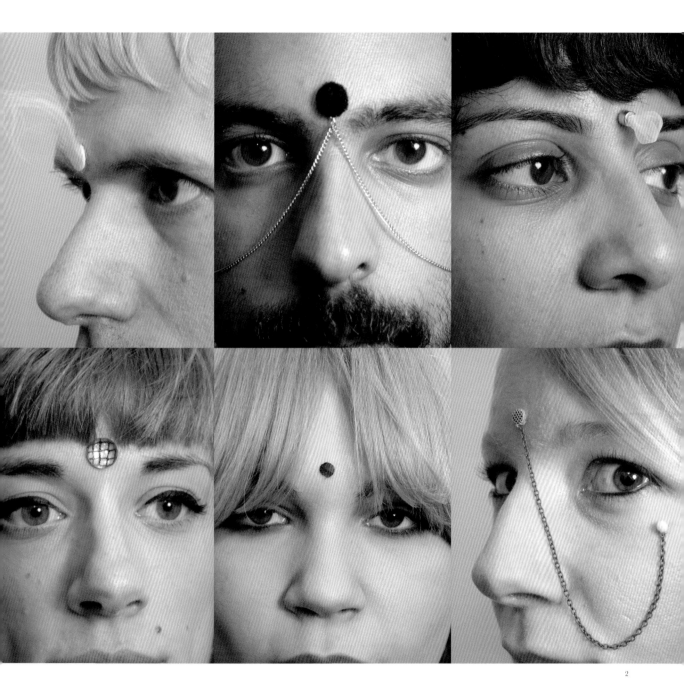

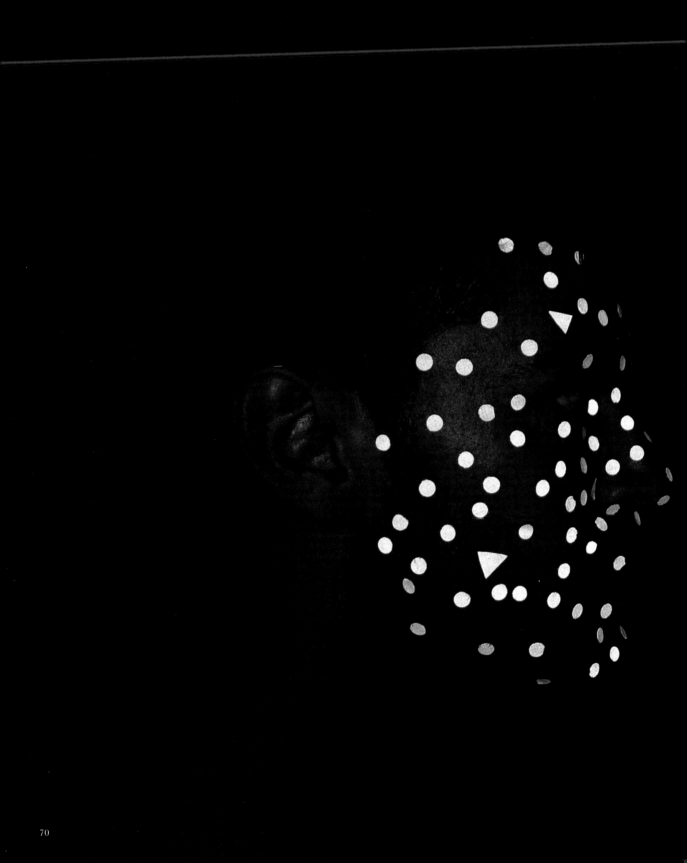

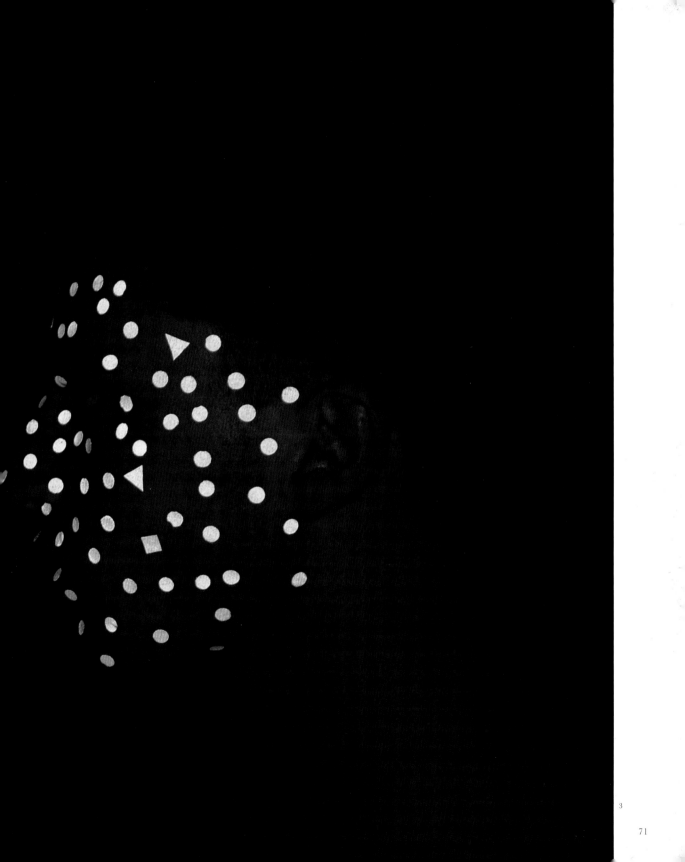

VINTAGE INVITE

The invitation draws inspirations from the client's store identity based on lines. Two images with words are broken up into strips and spaced out alternatively, allowing recipients of the invite to read 'VINTAGE' on one side and 'INVITE' on the other when it is folded into a concertina. Detailed information is layed out on the back.

Design: Adrian Newell Client: Vintage Type of Work: Invitation
Year: 2006

Angle-Distance Adapt   ◀ *P.62*   ☛ *P.94*

ZIEK 10.11
27.04

tussenlichaamengee

Museum Dr. Guislain   *tentoonstelli*
De Bijloke Muziekcentrum Gent   *concerten*
STAM / Gent Cultuurstad   *lezingen en d*

INFORMATIE

ZIEK *10.11.'07–*
27.04.'08

tussenlichaamengeest.be

Museum Dr. Guislain   *tentoonstelling*
De Bijloke Muziekcentrum Gent   *concerten*
STAM / Gent Cultuurstad   *lezingen en debat*

INFORMATIE: t 09 216 35 95

ZIEK 10.11.'07– 27.04.'08
tussenlichaamengeest.be
Museum Dr. Guislain
De Bijloke Muziekcentrum Gent
ent Cultuurstad
tentoonstelling
concerten
lezingen en debat
INFORMATIE: t 09 216 35 95

ZIEK, TUSSEN LICHAAM EN GEEST

The overprint of a mentally ill person to a seemingly so-called normal person symbolises the title of exhibition 'Ziek, tussen lichaam en geest' (Sick, between body and mind). Bizarre and whimsical, the poster provokes curiosity and invites people to learn about sicknesses that are common in modern world.

TATTOO ICONS

Not only as eye-catching as it is, the unique reddish plastic slipcase helps to reveal the 'two-faced' graphics on each side of the book cover. The overlapping images immediately come alive when the book goes in and out of the case. The idea is to make the book even more playful and interactive, accomplishing the experimental nature of the entire project.

Design: viction:workshop ltd. Client: viction:ary Type of Work:
Publication Year: 2006

Process-Interact   P.74   P.78

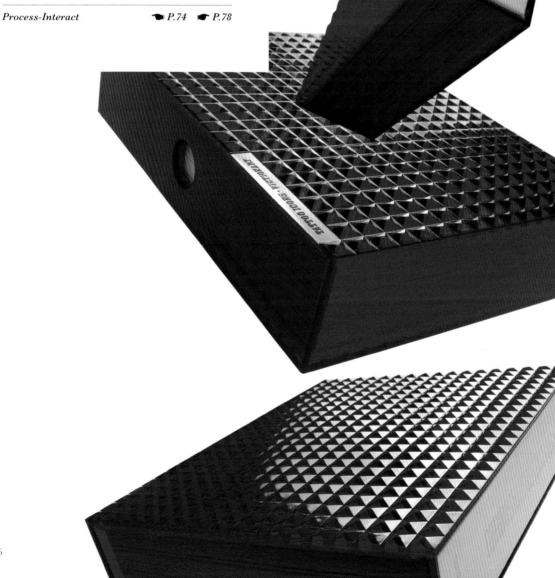

GRAPHIC KNOWLEDGE

Ward was thinking of some information system that were visually complex but simple in reality, and he came up with this filtering system that offers the opportunity to show only the information you wanted. The system works with a red-and-blue filter, which he calls the 'boomerang.' He uses it to switch between information quickly.

Design: Vaughan Ward Client: Vaughan Ward Type of Work: Book Year: 2007

Process-Interact   *P.76*   *P.82*

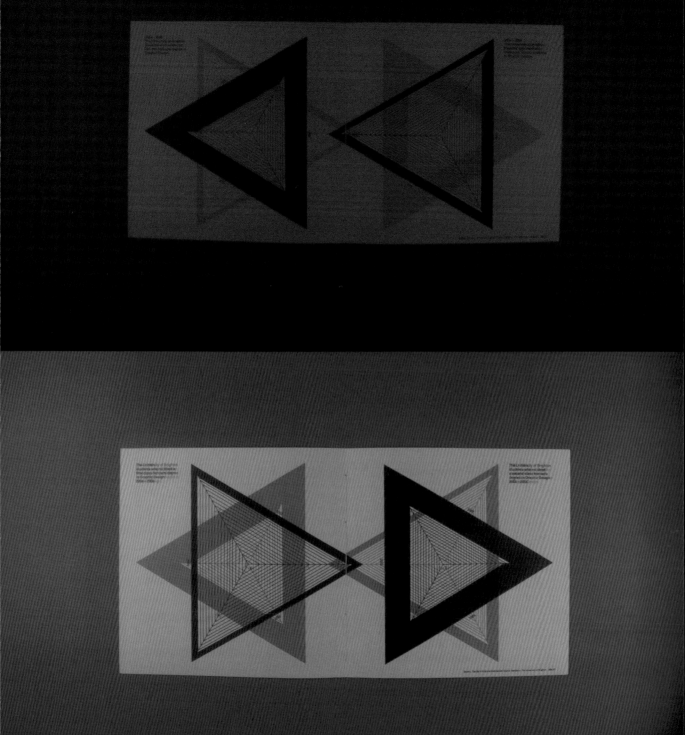

GR-O-
APH-
IC GE

KNO-
WLE-
DGE

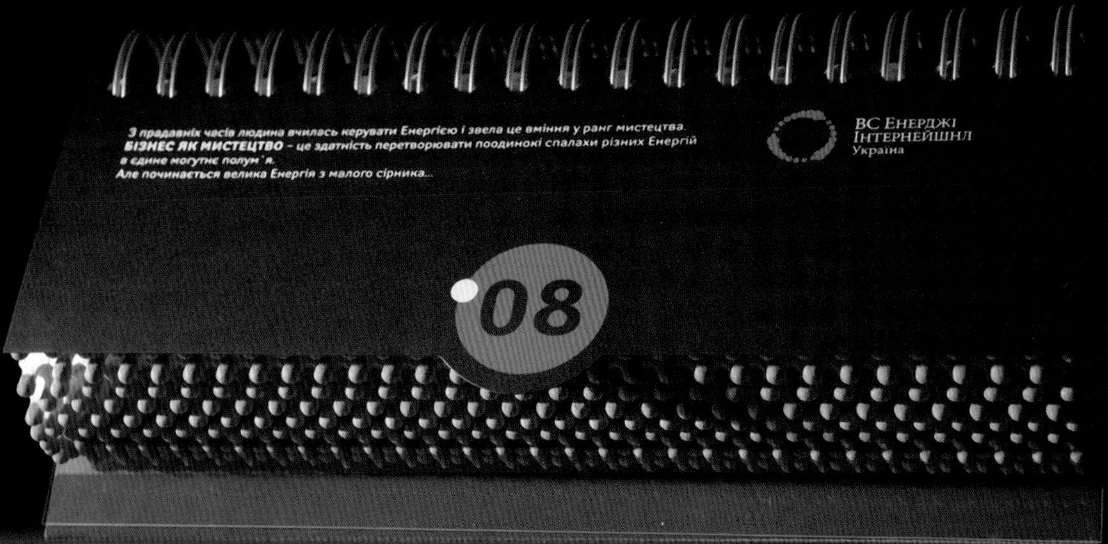

З прадавніх часів людина вчилась керувати Енергією і звела це вміння у ранг мистецтва. **БІЗНЕС ЯК МИСТЕЦТВО** – це здатність перетворювати поодинокі спалахи різних Енергій в єдине могутнє полум'я. Але починається велика Енергія з малого сірника...

ВС Енерджі Інтернейшнл
Україна

°08

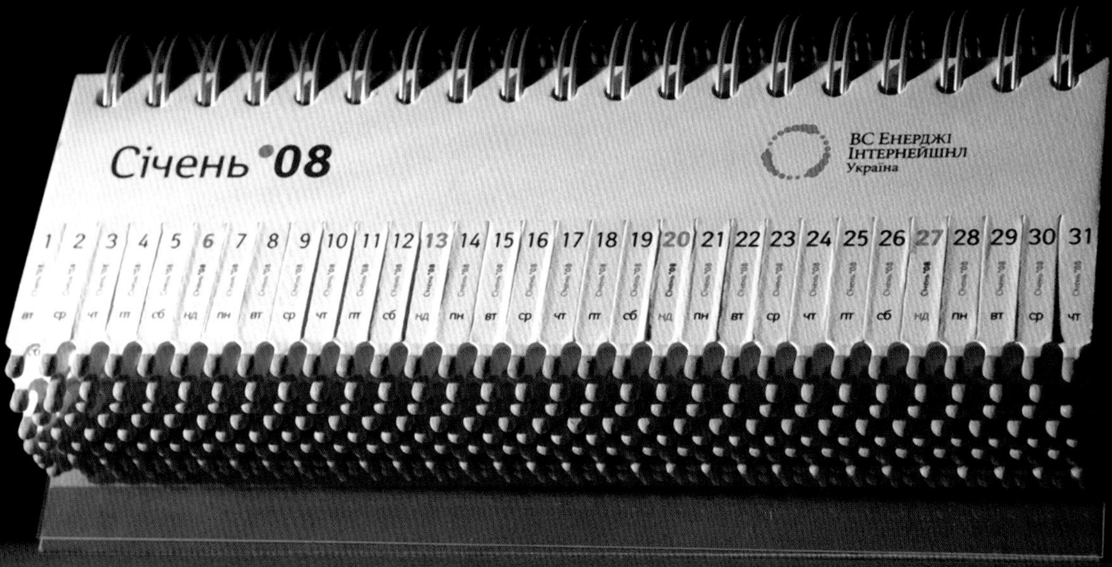

Січень °08

ВС Енерджі Інтернейшнл
Україна

| 1 | 2 | 3 | 4 | 5 | 6 | 7 | 8 | 9 | 10 | 11 | 12 | 13 | 14 | 15 | 16 | 17 | 18 | 19 | 20 | 21 | 22 | 23 | 24 | 25 | 26 | 27 | 28 | 29 | 30 | 31 |

CALENDAR MADE OF MATCHES

'Energy' is important in every aspect, and this calendar is made to celebrate that kind of strength and vitality. Each toothed page represents a month while days are the numbered matches. Matches have been dipped in a special chemical solution and covered with sulphur. The striking surfaces are laid on both sides of the stand base.

Design: Graphic design studio by Yurko Gutsulyak Client: VS Energy International Ukraine Type of Work: Calendar Year: 2007-08

Process-Interact   *P.78* *P.84*

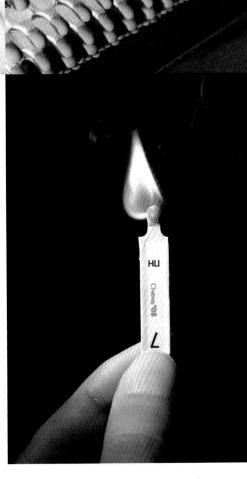

CREEP.

A set of three type-based posters is created to promote a horror film festival held in Manchester, UK. In order to stay away from the generic and clichés of the horror genre, a Swiss-style typography is adopted. The cropped text at the top and bottom refers to the 'rolling' title credits shown at the end of a film.

Design: Face37 Client: D&AD Type of Work: Poster Year: 2007

Process-Interact ☞ *P.82* ☞ *P.92*

A
Sean S.
Cunningham
Film—
Friday the 13th

Jason

Creep.
Horror Film Festival
Friday the 13th
15. August — 26. August 2007

Director: Sean S. Cunningham
Writer: Victor Miller
Producer: Sean S. Cunningham

Tickets & Information:
0131 229 2550

www.filmfest.co.uk

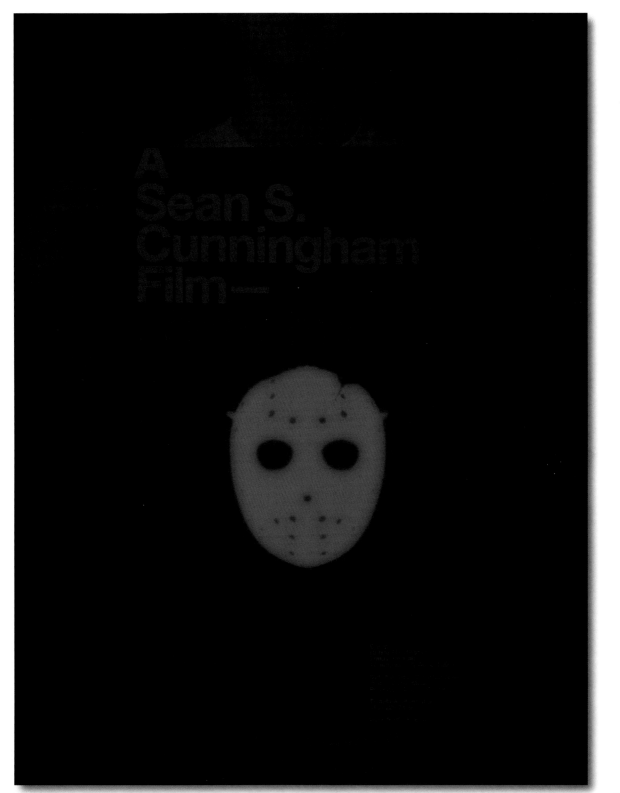

A
Sean S.
Cunningham
Film

FLAT LIFE

The Flat Life series containing Flat Light[1] and Flat Time[2] was the result of borrowing an Anglepoise task light from college. Magee was amazed at how it lent an atmosphere of productivity and efficiency on his desk to the room, and wondered if just an image of the light would be enough to create this atmosphere. The project led to seeing if the image could also be made to function as a light.

Design: Finn Magee Client: SUCK UK Type of Work: Functional poster
Year: 2007

Look-Alikes ☛ *P.53* ☛ *P.90*

2.

LIQUID BOOKMARK

Each of these bookmarks is handmade by the designer himself. The 'liquid' paint dangles when it is used to mark your place in the book. Each design is a one-off.

Design: Kyouei design Client: Kyouei design Type of Work: Bookmark Year: 2008

Look-Alikes   *P.88*   *P.103*

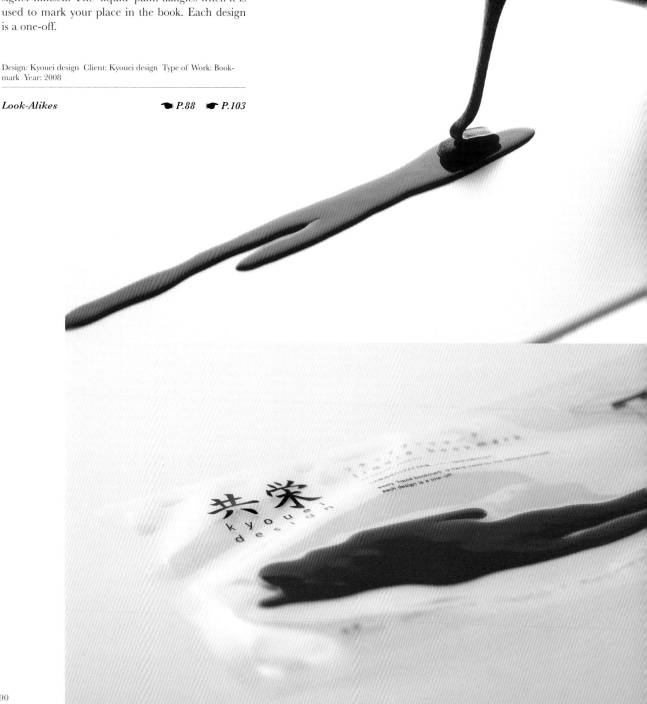

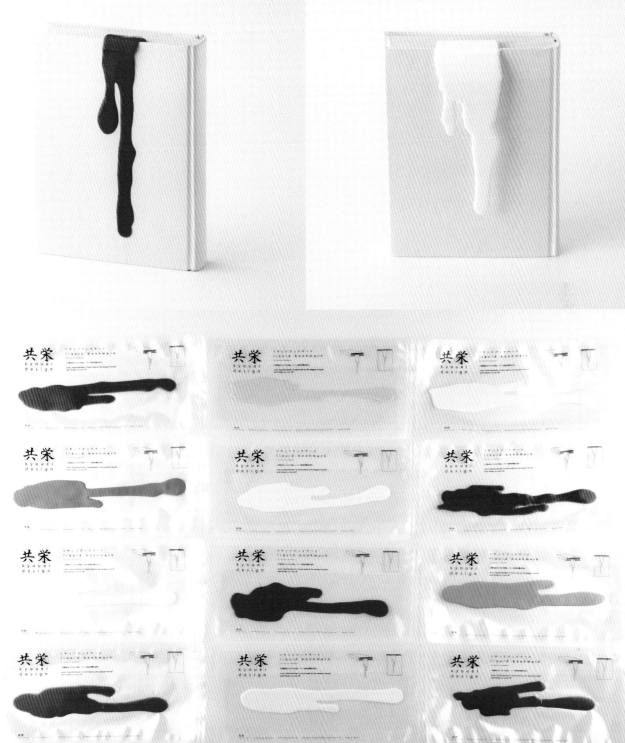

THE CHASE CALENDAR

The Chase's wall calendar makes virtue of necessity. It provides a witty graphic solution to the problem of string intrusion by merging the hanging string with visual illusions relative to every month of a year.

Design: The Chase Illustration: Mark Blade Typography: Abi Stones Client: The Chase Type of Work: Calendar Year: 2007

Process-Interact   *P.84*   *P.96*

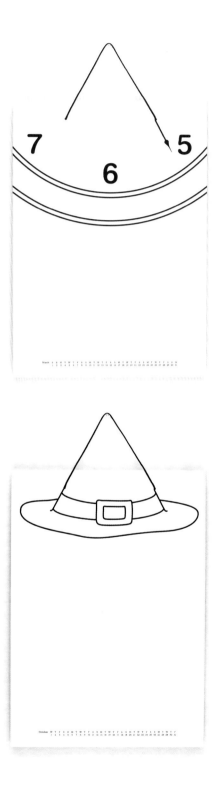

Merry Christmas and a Happy New Year from The Chase

DECORATION

This calendar has two sheets identically printed with dates for each month. The one with die cuts overlaps and complements the other in relief when the calendar is hung on the wall.

Design: DRAFT Co., Ltd Client: D-BROS Type of Work: Calendar
Year: 2004

Angle-Distance Adapt 🐦 *P.72* ☜ *P.100*

RAIN POSITIVE

Rain Positive aims to persuade people to look at rain in a different way. Unique printing process is employed so that posters could only reveal their messages when exposed to the rain.

Design: us design studio Client: us design studio Type of Work: Poster Year: 2007

Process-Interact   ☛ *P.92*   ☛ *P.98*

ZOOM IN ZOOM OUT

The book celebrates the versatility of today's designers and kicks off with a title printed with a subtle effect. Either words 'IN' or 'OUT' could only be revealed with the aid of the striped board that goes with the book. The cover design hints the readers to look at the collection in a different manner.

Design: viction:workshop ltd. Client: viction:ary Type of Work: Publication Year: 2006

Process-Interact   *P.96*   *P.104*

GIVE AND TAKE

Having the concept 'give and take' evolved out of personal emotions experienced during the year while suiting perfectly to the Christmas theme, Schmidt uses black and white triangles of various sizes to convey the idea and construct a classic Christmas tree to be recognised within a certain distance. The product can be served as a wrapping paper-cum-greeting card.

Design: Nikolaus Schmidt Graphic Design & Typography Client: Nikolaus Schmidt Graphic Design & Typography Type of Work: Greeting card Year: 2005

Angle-Distance Adapt　　　🖝 *P.94*　🖝 *P.102*

FLAT BULB

The flat bulb is slimmer than usual bulbs. The duo believes bulbs had to be round only because the way they were blown and moulded, which helped creating a vacuum inside. However, flat bulbs now share more advantages – they are smaller in size and thus cost less for transportation. It's less likely to break them by rolling off the table too.

Design: Joon & June Client: Joon & June Type of Work: Bulb Year: 2008

Angle-Distance Adapt *P.100* *P.142*

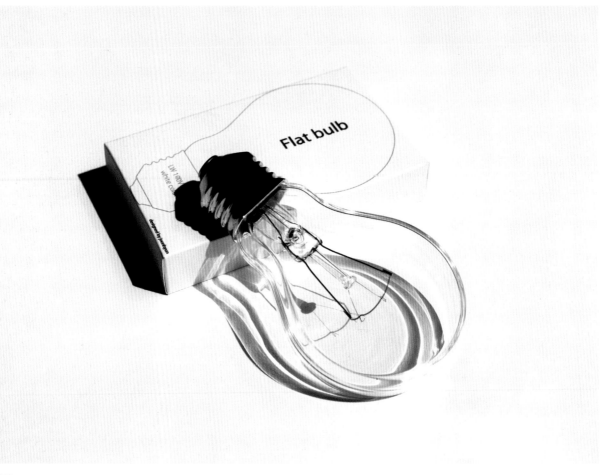

BULB LANTERN

Handmade by a Japanese craftsman, Bulb Lantern takes the shape of classic light bulbs and lights up the room like the real ones. These latterns are created for the designboom mart in Furniture Fair in Stockholm, 2008.

Design: Kyouei design Client: Kyouei design Type of Work: Lamp
Year: 2008

Look-Alikes　　　🖝 *P.90*　🖝 *P.108*

EUROCITIES

There was a big event in Barcelona where mayors from different European cities were invited to exchange views and future projects. The event was made less formal while socially more interesting by inviting guests to leave opinions, drawings, photographs impressions and feelings on the interactive tablecloth.

Art Direction: CLOUD 9 Design: POLAR Client: Ajuntament de Barcelona (Barcelona City Hall) Type of Work: Tablecloth Year: 2002

Process-Interact *P.98* *P.110*

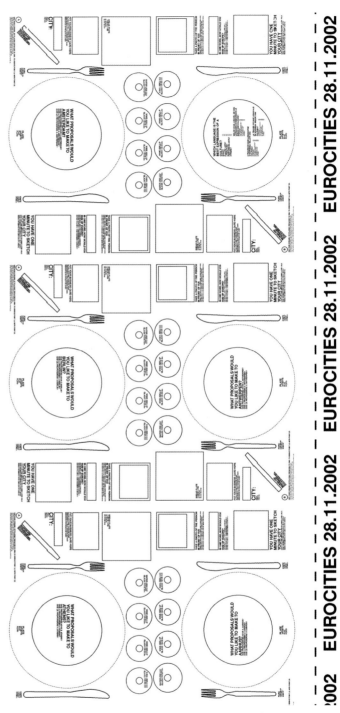

MESSY

AZE Design finds people nowadays treat dining only an activity to satisfy hunger and forget the pleasure of celebrating meals. Patterns on **MESSY** illustrates a situation where people would spend time together for a meal, bringing back the conception of mealtime.

Design: AZE Design Photography: Monika Filipiuk Client: AZE Design Type of Work: Tablecloth Year: 2006

Look-Alikes 🐀 *P.103* 🐀 *P.113*

[SHIKISAI] VENETIAN BLINDS

The string is not a print, but a real one, which you can pull to open the blinds. The shirt allows you to enjoy a cool breeze in the very warm summer.

Design: Noto Fusai Client: Noto Fusai Type of Work: T-shirt Year: 2006

Process-Interact　　　　　　　　🐭 *P.104*　🖝 *P.112*

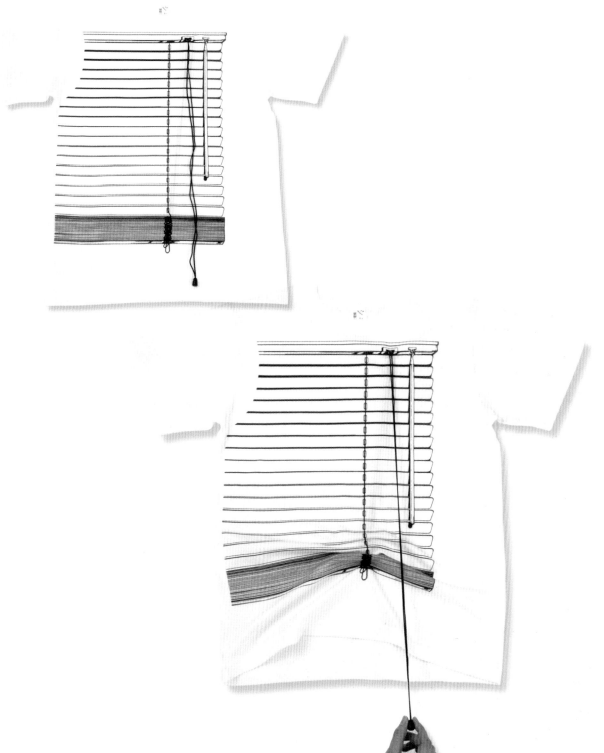

CHANGING LANES

Two great wine regions, two talented wine makers, one new wine – using grapes from the Margaret River and McLaren Vale for one wine has never been done before. The face on the label changes from Mark Lane to Justin Lane, the two wine makers, as the bottle is tilted.

Design: Mash Client: Redheads Wine Studio Type of Work: Wine bottle label Year: 2008

Process-Interact *P.110* *P.116*

POLAROID MIRROR

ATYPYK finds Polaroid pictures full of imperfections and that is why they are so beautiful, just as human beings. Here, POLAROID MIRROR has inherited the quality too.

Design: ATYPYK Client: ATYPYK Type of Work: Mirror Year: 2006

Look-Alikes　　　☞ *P.108*　☞ *P.114*

ANTI-THEFT CAR / BIKE DEVICE

These rust and scratch stickers are designed to make beautiful bikes/cars look rusted and scratched so that passing thieves would assume it's not worth stealing due to its apparent shabbyness. Wilcox has tried them on his own shiney new bike and confirmed that it has not been stolen after 13 days of experiment in London. Though, the anti-theft device is not guaranteed to work in any way.

Design: Dominic Wilcox Client: Dominic Wilcox Type of Work: Stickers
Year: 2007

Look-Alikes 🖰 *P.113* 🖰 *P.118*

Anti-Theft Bike/Car Device
These rust and scratch stickers
are designed to make your
beautiful bike (or car) look
rusted and scratched so that a
passing thief assumes the
vehicle is not worth stealing due
to its apparent shabbyness."

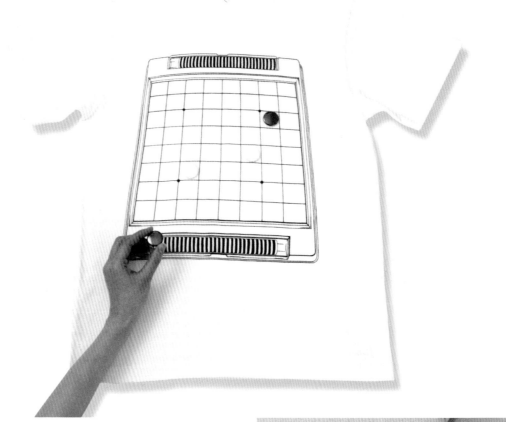

[SHIKISAI] REVERSI

'Reversi' or 'Othello' is a popular family game for children to learn the hierarchical relationship in Japanese sosiety. A standard eight-by-eight square grid is printed on T-shirt and you are free to arrange where to place the black and white pin badges.

Design: Noto Fusai Client: Noto Fusai Type of Work: T-shirt Year: 2007

Process-Interact   🖤 *P.112*   🖤 *P.117*

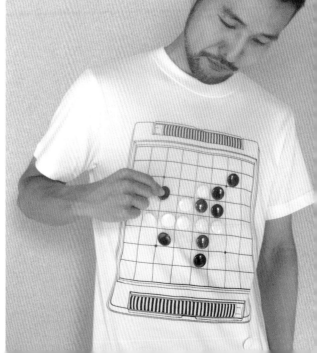

T-SHIRT 2009

Reveal your everyday habit by filling up the boxes of the silkscreened 2009 calendar. A pen is attached to the tee so that you could colour the box of the day when you wear it. See how you did by the end of 2009!

Design: Petter Hanberger Client: Petter Hanberger Type of Work: T-shirt print, Calendar Year: 2008

Process-Interact    *P.116*   *P.122*

117

HOPE FOREVER
BLOSSOMING

These inflatable vases are made from plastic bags used for shampoo refills. With the aid of thermo-compression technique, the vases are shaped to look like a real one made from glass when you pour water into it.

Design: DRAFT Co., Ltd Client: D-BROS Type of Work: Vase
Year: 2004-08

Look-Alikes   ☛ *P.114*   ☛ *P.124*

COLOURING DRESS

Colouring dress is an exclusive design for exhibition 'Daar' held to give tribute to the famous textile factory 'De Ploeg.' The black-and-white dress is provided with a set of textile markers, with which the wearer could use to colour the dress to her liking. The dress is a translation of possibilities and dreams that exist in everyone's life.

Design: Berber Soepboer (fashion), Michiel Schuurman (graphic) Client: "Daar" Exhibition Type of Work: Dress Year: 2008

Process-Interact *P.117* *P.130*

COOL SHADE TAPE

Cool shade tape is an extension to body tapes (P.126-127) and garment tapes (P.128-129) released in previous seasons. Sunglasses of distinctive styles, such as supermodel[1], disk jockey[2], architect and intellectual, are printed on adhesive tapes allowing varieties for easy styling.

Design: Azumi and David (A'N'D) Client: Azumi and David (A'N'D)
Type of Work: Printed adhesive tape Year: 2008

Look-Alikes

P.118   P.126

BODY TAPE

Azumi and David (A'N'D) wanted to create a product that could be worn as an accessory or used to accessorise or style an outfit, so they produced a series of adhesive tapes printed with elegant bracelets, belts and watches. The style of illustrations is inspired by Victorian catalogues and newspaper advertisements.

Design: Azumi and David (A'N'D) Client: Azumi and David (A'N'D)
Type of Work: Printed adhesive tape Year: 2007

Look-Alikes ☞ *P.124* ☞ *P.128*

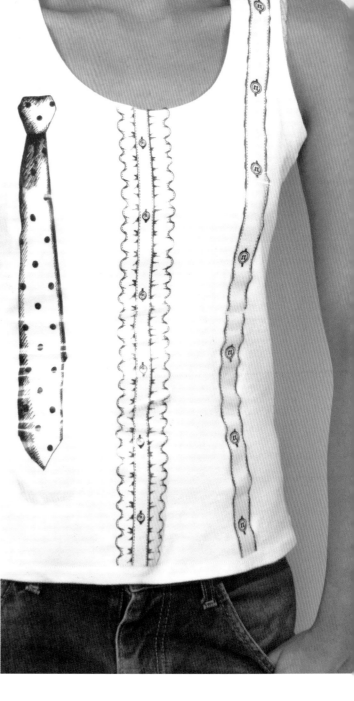

GARMENT TAPE

As an extension to Spring/Summer 2007 Body Tapes (P.126-127), another series of styling tapes are produced with alternative accessories, such as buttons, frills, ribbon bows and ties. The style of illustration is referenced by Victorian catalogues and newspaper advertisements.

Design: Azumi and David (A'N'D) Client: Azumi and David (A'N'D) Type of Work: Printed adhesive tape Year: 2008

Look-Alikes   ☞ *P.126*   ☞ *P.140*

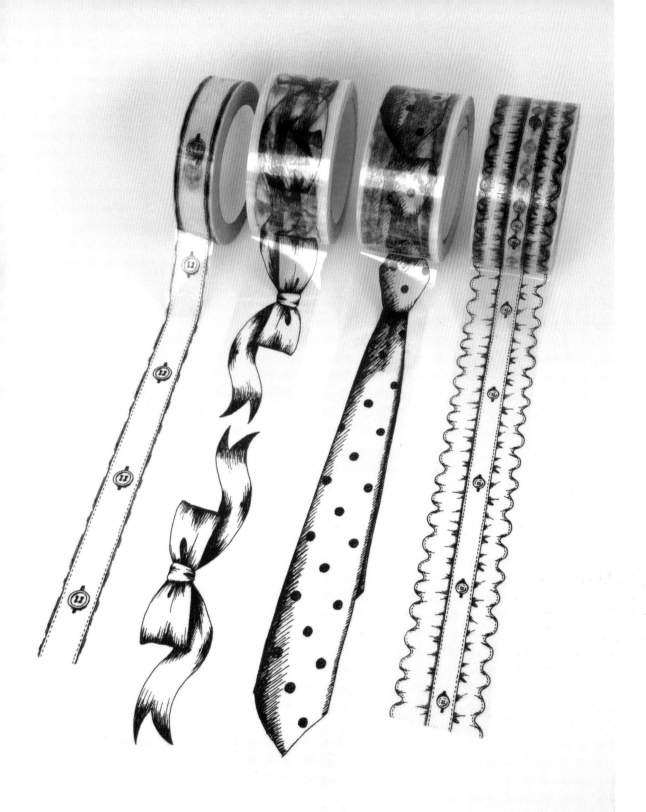

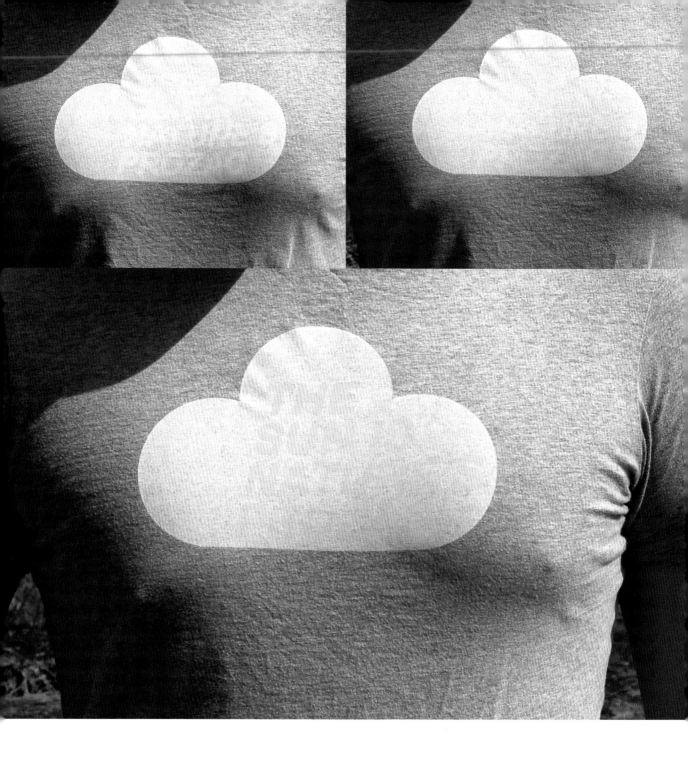

S.A.D. T-SHIRT

Hancox designed the S.A.D. T-shirts for one of his friends who was suffering from seasonal affective disorder (S.A.D.). The one with text screen-printed in UV sensitive ink is responsive to sunlight, while the other with a sun is overprinted with black heat-sensitive ink. The dark cloud would turn transparent at 32°C.

Design: Keith Hancox Client: -- Type of Work: T-shirt Year: 2008

Process-Interact 👆 *P.122* 👆 *P.132*

RAIN POSITIVE

Rain Positive aimed to persuade people to look at rain in a different way. Unique printing process was employed so that messages on the T-shirts could only be revealed when exposed to rain.

Design: us design studio Client: us design studio Type of Work: T-shirt
Year: 2007

Process-Interact   ☛ *P.130*   ☛ *P.180*

DESTRUCTIF MODERNIZATION

The custom-shaped mirror was specially made and mounted at a corner of the exterior wall of a museum for the exhibition 'Moje Twoje Miasto' (My, your city) in Lodz, Poland. The mirror was visible upon entry to the exhibition.

Design: Jan Vormann Client: Book Art Museum of Contemporary Art Repository, Lodz, Poland Type of Work: Mirror Year: 2007

Bounce-Off Appeal

☛ *P.38*   ☛ *P.196*

I HEART CLIPART.

I Heart Clipart is about the things that came along with
the advent of computers and technology in relationship
to visual aesthetics. It is an exploration into the balance
of this particularly polarised binary. It is also, in particular, a product of nostalgia.

Design: Alan Woo Client: Alan Woo Type of Work: Experimental Year:
2008

Pixel-Like
🖦 *P.42*   ☛ *P.138*

REFLECTIONS POSTER

This poster explores the nature of design excess and its implicit irony, exemplifying the snowball effect that occurs in the stylistic trends of design. It ideologically focuses on the prototypal nature of the image. It functions more as a commentary than a critique.

Design: Aesthetically Loyal Client: Aesthetically Loyal Type of Work: Poster Year: 2007

Blend-In Dizzy 🖝 *P.66*   🖝 *P.172*

DESKTOP

Eškinja's compositions are two-dimensional, perfectly treated in the details using simplicity to create metaphors and symbologies. In a world made of images, perceptive habits and fossilisation of the external relationships, Eškinja creates illusion of reality with materials well-related to the context he wants to create.

Artwork: Igor Eškinja Client: -- Type of Work: Installation Year: 2006

Pixel-Like 🖝 *P.136* 🖝 *P.158*

TEMPORARY CITY BENCH

This 'bench cover' showing a bench in a mature forest was produced for the benches in a barren, temporary park. The series of five designs picturing different moments of the day allows citizens of Rotterdam to discuss their day during their walk in the park. Temporary City Bench was a student project made in Willem de Kooning Academy, Rotterdam.

Design: Ohyescoolgreat. Client: Willem de Kooning Academy, Rotterdam
Type of Work: Product Year: 2007

Look-Alikes   ☞ *P.128*   ☞ *P.144*

WE HATE GRAVITY

We Hate Gravity examines the possibilities, the limitations and the use of space. What if there was no gravity? The state of weightlessness was built with the floor and props and realised through the camera lens. No Photoshop or any other retouching software processing was involved.

Design: Studio-SM Client: Studio-SM Type of Work: Photography Year: 2007

Angle-Distance Adapt

🐦 *P.102*   🐦 *P.152*

«BRICK WALL» ROLL DOWN CURTAIN

A very simple way to get your privacy back at home whenever you want – wall up your window by rolling down the 'BRICK WALL!'

Design: ATYPYK Client: ATYPYK Type of Work: Prototype Year: 2006

Look-Alikes   ☛ *P.140* ☛ *P.146*

LIQUID LAMP

Liquid Lamp made of iron plate appears to be an upside down container with liquid paint flowing down. There are two types of the lamp: Table and Bracket. The lamp is a collaboration between DSC corp. and Kyouei design.

Design: Kyouei design Client: DCS corp. Type of Work: Lamp Year: 2008

Look-Alikes   📎 *P.144*   📎 *P.147*

«OOOPS» TABLE MAT

Ruin your table with paint stains. What a nice start to eat properly!

Design: ATYPYK Client: ATYPYK Type of Work: Prototype
Year: 2006

Look-Alikes ☛ *P.146* ☛ *P.148*

RITA'S LIVING ROOM

Rita's living room represents the typical Quebec living room, in the style of mixed trends throughout the years with the use of archetypical decoration and layout. Far from modern condo-style loft and living rooms that cover the pages of hip magazines, this living room could be yours. The room installation is now possessed by Musée National des Beaux-Arts du Québec.

Design: Rita Client: Rita Type of Work: Installation Year: 2006

Look-Alikes   ☛ *P.147*   ☛ *P.154*

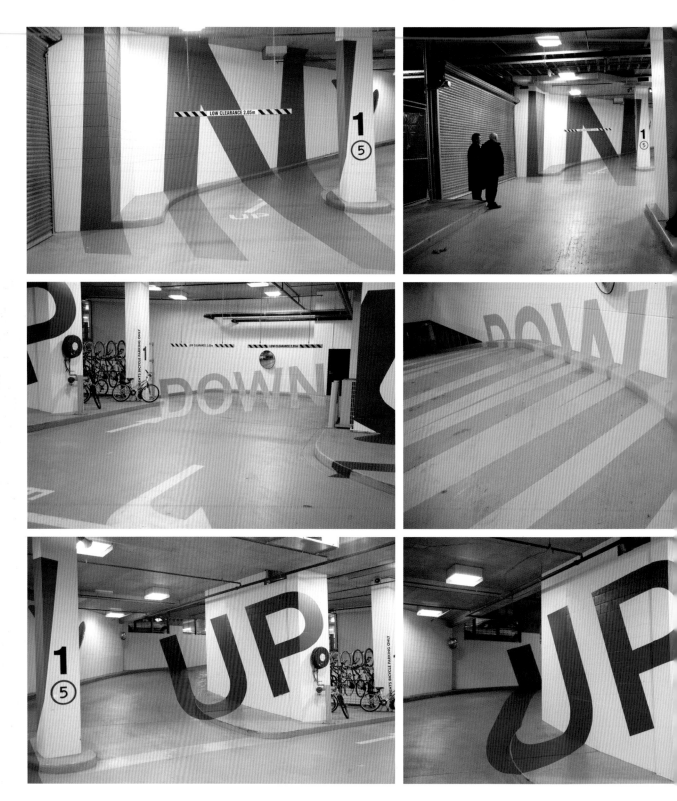

EUREKA TOWER
CAR-PARK MELBOURNE

Distorted letters on the walls of the Eureka Tower Car-park can only be read perfectly at the right positions, where information is most relevant for visitors to navigate. Peemöller produced the way-finding system when he was with emerystudio.

Design: Axel Peemöller Design Client: emerystudio, Melbourne Type of Work: Architectural graphics, Way-finding Year: 2006

Angle-Distance Adapt   ☛ *P.142*   ☛ *P.156*

PUMA BREAKOUT

Puma has created a breakout of fashion onto the streets and in turn make the sporting world more stylish and fun. With the ultraviolet paws of puma, the campaign went on throughout the night.

Design: Alex Woolley Client: Puma D&AD student brief Type of Work: Marketing campaign Year: 2007

Look-Alikes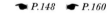 🐾 *P.148* 🐾 *P.160*

CHAIR 1

Mrsnik thinks design is about making chairs and likes to apply her illustrations to a three-dimentional profile. Producing objects with a known function doesn't interest her much. Chair 1 was indeed a very solid chair made of tapes.

Design: Nina Mrsnik Client: Nina Mrsnik Type of Work: Product Year: 2008

Angle-Distance Adapt   ☛ *P.152*   ☛ *P.192*

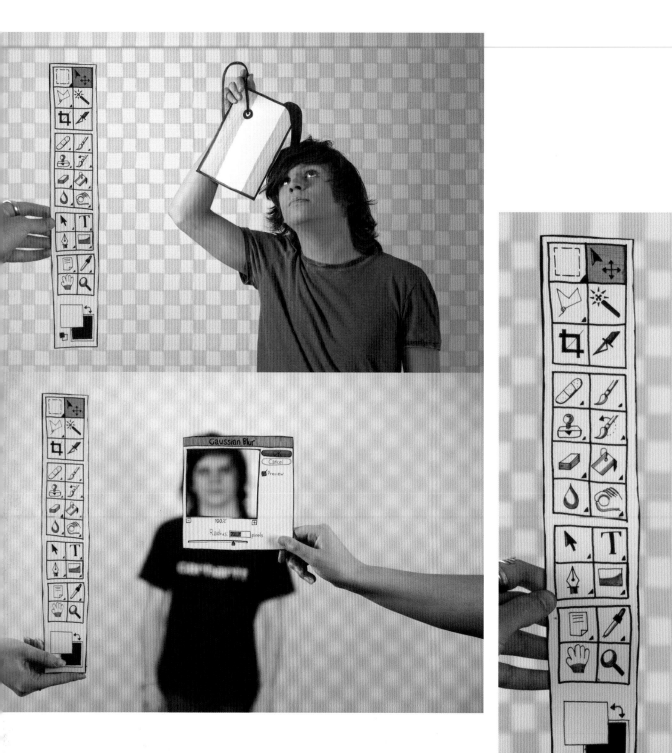

TELL A LIE

Both Cornish and Hadlow are interested in 'unspecial effects' – to make great graphic work with just their minds, hands and traditional techniques with no computer aids. Cornish first came up with the idea of mimicking common Photoshop tricks 'in camera,' drawing on the tradition of famous French photographer Henri Cartier-Bresson. They worked together on the hand-drawn look and photography.

Design: Ed Cornish, Henry Hadlow Photography: Henry Hadlow Model: Ed Cornish Client: Ed Cornish, Henry Hadlow Type of Work: Photography satire Year: 2008

Pixel-Like   *P.138*   *P.162*

LITTLE PEOPLE
PROJECT

Since 2006, 'Little People' has come alive and began to mimic city-dwellers at insignificant street corners of London through miniature model train set characters. The street-based side of Slinkachu's work plays with the notion of surprise. Titles given to these scenes and the scenes themselves, which are more evident through photography, reflect the loneliness and melancholy of living in a big city, almost being lost and overwhelmed.

Design: Slinkachu Client: Slinkachu Type of Work: Photography, Street installation Year: 2006-08

Look-Alikes
🐦 *P.154*　🐦 *P.166*

PiXXXEL

Lemoigne was given a free hand to do a fashion shoot for a magazine. Pixelised models was the primary idea but he needed a strong impact with it. He then looked for a subject or form that is usually hidden by pixels and pornography was what he thought could make a perfect connection to the magazine theme.

Design: Jean-Yves Lemoigne Client: Amusement magazine Type of Work: Photography Year: 2008

Pixel-Like   🐦 *P.158*

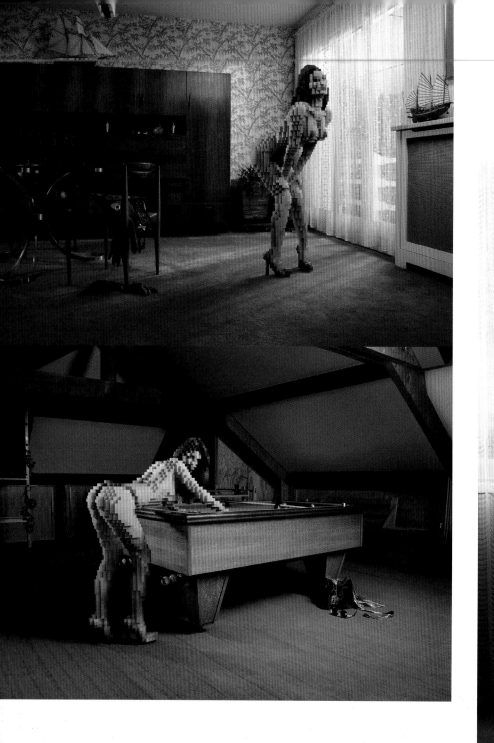

by:Larm 21-23 FEBRUARY 2008   OSLO NORWAY

BY:LARM 2008

Rune Mortensen Design Studio was invited to create a new profile for by.Larm 2008, the biggest music conference in Scandinavia. The event happened in Oslo, Norway and the concept is about bringing music to the streets.

Design: Rune Mortensen Design Studio Photography: Rune Mortensen Design Studio Client: Bureau Storm Type of Work: Poster Year: 2007

Look-Alikes 🖝 *P.160* 🖝 *P.170*

by:Larm 21-23 FEBRUARY 2008 OSLO NORWAY

IT'S NOT HAPPENING HERE. BUT IT IS HAPPENING NOW. amnesty international

NOT HERE BUT NOW

Amnesty International's primary mission is to campaign against the worldwide abuse of human rights. 'Not here but now' was designed to raise awareness among people in Switzerland with real examples of the worldwide human rights abuse directly brought to people's eyes. Two worlds collided on 200 individual posters, each of which is meticulously merged with its specific surroundings.

Creative Direction: Pius Walker Art Direction: Marianne Friedli Design: Christian Bachofer Photography: Federico Naef Client: Amnesty International Type of Work: Poster Year: 2006-07

Look-Alikes

☛ P.166   ☛ P.198

WARPING WALLPAPER

Warping Wallpaper blurs the border between architectural wall structures and interior decorations by adapting patterns to the particular infrastructure of a room. So now, doors, light switches, painting and wallpaper don't bang together but exist in a rather bizarre harmony.

Design: surrealien Client: Museum für Kunst und Gewerbe Hamburg Type of Work: Wallpaper Year: 2008

Blend-In Dizzy

P.137   P.174

LYDMAR HOTEL 617

This project depicts the interior design of one room inside a design hotel done for the art event, 'Tokyo Style in Stockholm.' In the room, besides architecture, there were also the bed linen and yukata (Japanese bathrobes). Setting off with such direction, Atelier Bow-Wow proposed to cover all surfaces with a single designed pattern that eliminates the silhouettes of all elements.

Design: Atelier Bow-Wow Textile: Yoko Ando Client: Tokyo Style in Stockholm Type of Work: Interior, Textile Year: 2004

Blend-In Dizzy  *P.172* *P.176*

WHEN BODY ART MEETS WALLPAPER

Since working with iconic Australian wallpaper artist Florence Broadhurst in 2005, Hack has been blending gorgeous models into their environments to play out the energy of selected wallpapers. Models in Hack's works were entirely painted in patterns of Broadhurst's wallpapers creating seamless illusions to human eyes. Respective art prints featured here are Evolution Crocodile[1] with Broadhurst's 'Crocodile Skin' wallpaper, Wallpaper Tawny Frogmouth[2] with Spotted Floral wallpaper, Wallpaper Carnation[3] with Carnation wallpaper and Wallpaper Owl[4] with Kabuki wallpaper.

Design: Emma Hack Client: Emma Hack Artist Type of Work: Body illustration, Photographic art print Year: 2008

Blend-In Dizzy

P.174   P.188

1

2

3

MAGIC DIARY

Tossed conversational pattern includes kittens, horses, lipsticks, cupcakes, bows and more. This hand-screened wallpaper employed multiple layers of invisible and fluorescent inks which only activate under a black light. Use the pen provided to write secret thoughts inside the speech bubbles. No worries – no one knows what's yours unless the black light is on.

Design: Breanne Trammell Client: Breanne Trammell Type of Work: Wallpaper
Year: 2007

Process-Interact   👁 *P.132*   👁 *P.184*

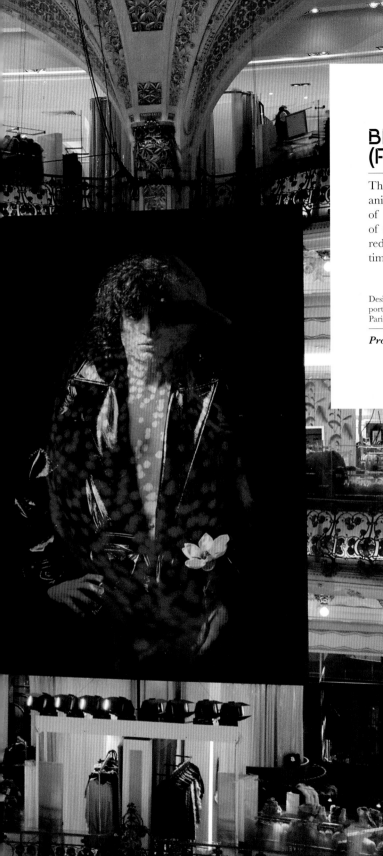

BETES DE MODE
(FASHION BEASTS)

Thirteen pictures made with fashion portraits in blue and animal portraits in red were displayed in the shop windows of Galeries Lafayette on boulevard Hausmann. A system of coloured gelatine on the window panes or the blue and red light projection made visible the fashion portrait sometimes and the animal portrait the other time.

Design: ©Helmo + Thomas Dimetto Photography: ©Laurent Croisier (Fashion portraits), ©Christophe Urbain (Animal portraits) Client: Galeries Lafayette, Paris Type of Work: Campaign installation Year: 2006

Process-Interact   ☜ *P.180*

WARPING WALLPAPER

Warping Wallpaper blurs the border between architectural wall structures and interior decorations by adapting patterns to the particular infrastructure of a room. So now, doors, light switches, painting and wallpaper don't bang together but exist in a rather bizarre harmony. Featured here is the Warping Wallpaper for the Ruby Lounge, London.

Art direction: David Knight Design: surrealien Client: Ruby Lounge Type of Work: Wallpaper Year: 2006

Blend-In Dizzy  *P.176* *P.190*

WARPING WALLPAPER

Warping Wallpaper blurs the border between architectural wall structures and interior decorations by adapting patterns to the particular infrastructure of a room. So now, doors, light switches, painting and wallpaper don't bang together but exist in a rather bizarre harmony. Featured here is the Warping Wallpaper for ENVY post-production Studio, London.

Art direction: David Knight Design: surrealien Client: ENVY post production
Type of Work: Wallpaper Year: 2007

Blend-In Dizzy

🖤 *P.188*   🖤 *P.206*

ONE PERCENT PRODUCTS @ INTERIOR LIFESTYLE TOKYO

The exhibition took place in an atrium that gave visitors a view from the second floor. Everything from sofas to plants were mounted on the wall so that viewers would feel as if they were on the first floor while looking down from the second floor, and as if they were looking down from above while standing on the ground floor. Visitors were essentially made to 'walk on the walls' and became part of the display, heightening the topsy-turvy effect.

Design: nendo Photography: Peter Saville Client: one percent products
Type of Work: Exhibition Year 2007

Angle-Distance Adapt   *P.156*   *P.202*

195

THE LEVEL TUNNEL BY HUSSEIN CHALAYAN VOL.08

The Level Tunnel by Hussein Chalayan is a world of its own, which can be experienced by viewing it from the outside and exploring it blindfolded from the inside. The art installation focuses on the unique taste of Level Vodka and intends to challenge beholders on many levels through the use of sound, smell and tactile materials.

Concept: Hussein Chalayan Design: Hussein Chalayan, Boys Don't Cry Client: Level Vodka / Absolut Vodka Type of Work: Interactive art installation Year: 2007-08

Bounce-Off Appeal

🖙 *P.134*

CITY VIEW

CITY VIEW is a permanent display on the second floor of Nanba Parks Tower, Osaka, Japan. The spotlit numbers scattered on the wall cast a silhouette of a woman leaning against the glass balustrade.

Design: Kumi Yamashita Client: Nankai Urban Development Co., Ltd Type of Work: Art installation Year: 2003

Look-Alikes   ☜ *P.170*   ☜ *P.200*

THE ART OF
LIGHT AND SHADES

These permanent displays relate the art of light and shades in different parts of Japan. GLIDER[1] at the entrance hall of Takikawa Hall, Hokkaido, casts the silhouette of a gliding girl when the thin metal intstallation is lit from above; FEATHER[2] at Akiru Municipal Medical Center, Tokyo, illustrates the profile of a girl holding her knees when the wooden panel is lit from below; CLOUD[3] exhibits a couple silhouetted against the wall on the third floor of Sapporo Stellar Place, Hokkaido, when the thin metal panel is lit from above.

Design: Kumi Yamashita Client: Takikawa Hall[1], Akiru Municipal Medical Center[2], Sapporo-Eki Sogo Kaihatsu Co., Ltd[3] Type of Work: Art installation Year: 2002[1], 2006[2], 2005[3]

Look-Alikes  *P.198*

たきかわホール

1

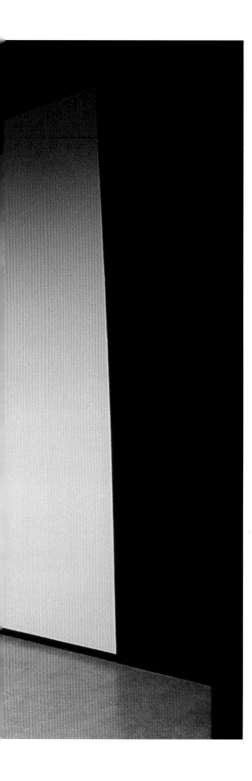

2

3

PAINTDROP SCULPTURES

Out of material discovery, Dorosz began to regard the primacy of paint drops, a form that takes shape purely from its own viscosity and the air it falls through. The 'stasis painting' was formed by trapping fallen paint drops in a grid work of vertical transparent rods. Through the viewer's movements in aligning and de-aligning these pixel-like paint drops, full body portrait emerges and vanishes.

Artwork: Chris Dorosz Client: Chris Dorosz Type of Work: Installation Year: 2008

Angle-Distance Adapt  *P.192* *P.214*

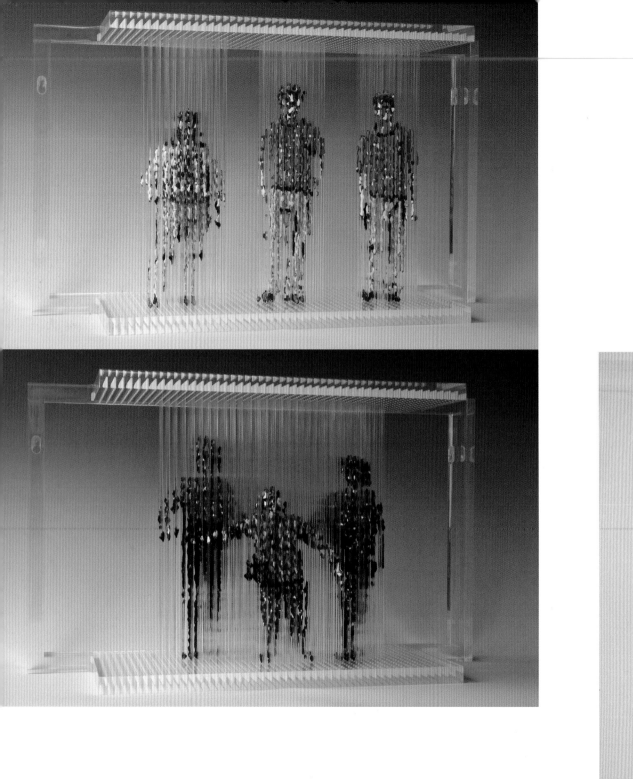

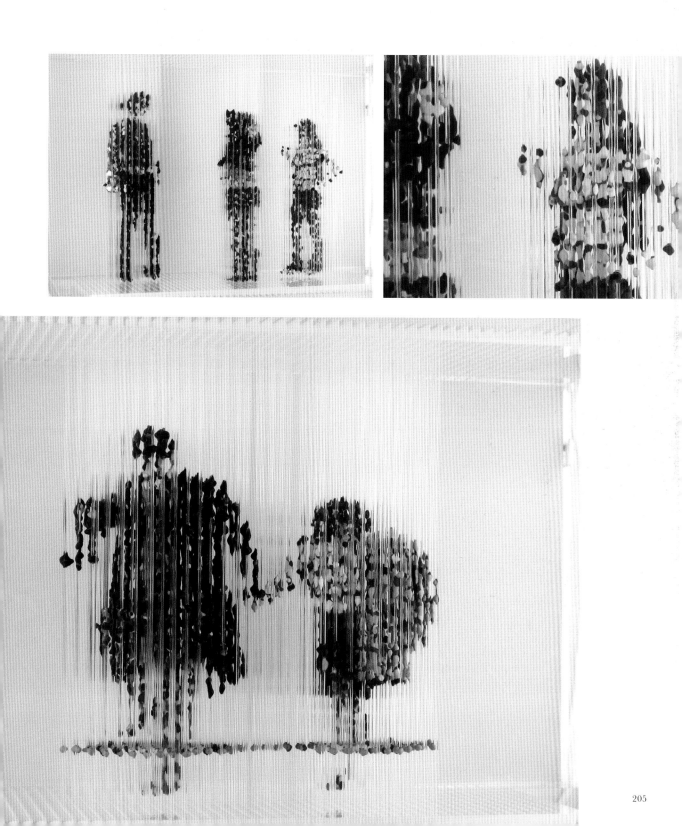

BLACK LIGHT

Artists Broersen and Lukacs engaged with an essential aspect of patterns in 'Black Light.' They pointed out the paradoxical situation that elements appearing successively in an indiscriminate series could simultaneously represent order and chaos. The idea behind the design was originated in moutainous terrain in Spain, where they noted the ambiguous yet symmetric and ordered nature of the indigenous plants.

Design: Persijn Broersen & Margit Lukács Client: Nieuwe Vide, Haarlem, The Netherlands Type of Work: Artwork Year: 2004

Blend-In Dizzy 🖝 *P.190*   🖝 *P.208*

POST HORIZON

Post Horizon depicts a horizon running through the Stedelijk Museum. The collage consists of hundreds of drawings, partly based on newspaper photos. These drawings were used as 'bricks' in the final structure.

Design: Persijn Broersen & Margit Lukács Client: Stedelijk Museum 's-Hertogenbosch, The Netherlands Type of Work: Mural collage Year: 2006

Blend-In Dizzy 👈 *P.206* 👈 *P.210*

MUSIC FOR PATTERNS

To play with viewers' perception of an architectural space, Music for Patterns covers the gallery entirely with vibrating optical patterns, which somehow seem to protrude from the walls. Visitors were invited to wear geometrically-patterned overalls specifically designed to blend into the installation. Minimal electronic sound by Ricardo Milho was produced to enhance the overall experience.

Design: Music for Patterns Client: Kingsgate Workshops Gallery Type of Work: Installation Year: 2008

Blend-In Dizzy

P.208

STEALTH

Stealth was originally designed to promote The Map Office at the opening of the 2007 summer season exhibitions at The Studio Museum in Harlem, a contemporary art institution that focuses on artists of African or African American descent. Map wanted to make a poster about invisibility, referencing a quote from the book 'Invisible Man' by the famous American novelist and former resident of Harlem, Ralph Ellison – I am invisible, understand, simply because people refuse to see me.'

Design: The Map Office (Eddie Opara, Ryan Lauer, Salvador Orara) Client: The Map Office Type of Work: Self promotion Year: 2008

Angle-Distance Adapt   ☛ *P.202*

SNAPSHOT CAMPAIGN: LET EYES AND BRAINS PLAY

Best 100 entries to Design • Play photo campaign from a cluster of fun-loving mortals, featuring the very first-hand eye-trick experiences spotted out of everyday occasions!

"Try for failure and you'll never be disappointed."
Carl David Leeth
Photographer & Photoshop Artist @ Spokane, USA

"Keep the spirit, raids in any idea, experiments and divertiser, the results that may be or not the desired but if you do not try not know. I am happy inventive."
Carlos Gonzalez Gavidia
Graphic Designer @ Caracas, Venezuela

"Please pass the Bauhaus."
Steve Rura & Tiziana Haug
Art Directors & Graphic Designers @ New York City, USA

"What is true is invisible to our eyes."
Elfi Chan & Genie Ngai
Flâneur @ Hong Kong, China

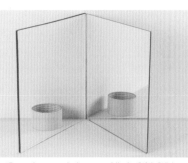

"Be curious, not judgemental." - by Walt Whitman
Hort
Design Studio @ Berlin, Germany

"Life must move on."
Ho Yan Yee
Editorial Assistant @ Hong Kong, China

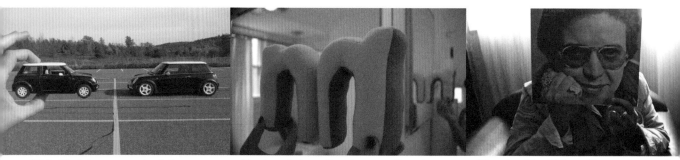

"Stick with whatever comes naturally."
Jonathan Sandridge
Graphic Designer @ Burlington (Vermont), USA

"Laugh at mistakes and love the process. Sleep when tired. Eat well. Dress in beautiful attire. Find a great hair stylist. Tricks are not just for kids. Believe wholeheartedly in everything you create. And honey, love is really a great feeling."
Jennifer Lew, Designer @ New York City, USA

"Keep the spirit, raids in any idea, experiments and divertiser, the results that may be or not the desired but if you do not try not know. I am happy inventive."
Carlos Gonzalez Gavidia
Graphic Designer @ Caracas, Venezuela

"Just let the monkey in you flow..."
Erik Geiger
Primary School Teacher @ Hong Kong, China

"Some laugh, some cry, but it's always a good thing to be made slightly less-self."
Freddie Yauner
Designer @ London, UK

"Please pass the Bauhaus."
Steve Rura & Tiziana Haug
Art Directors & Graphic Designers @ New York City, USA

"Looking at my kids sleeping makes me smile the stress of the day away."
Paul Farrington
Designer @ Brighton, UK

"Seeing is believing."
Dani Eveleigh, Lydia Cock-burnsmith
University Students @ Brighton, UK

"Fresh thoughts and perceptions can change the way people think."
Andrea Lorca
Photographer, Art Director & Designer @ São Paulo, Brazil

"It's better to regret something you did than something you didn't do."
Andreas Bense, University Student @ Copenhagen, Denmark

"Nothing's true, everything is permitted."
Sebastian Buur, Freelance Photographer @ Copenhagen, Denmark

"Ya Baha'u'l-Abha!"
George W. Hatcher
Aerospace Engineer @ Merritt Island, USA

219

PARQUE E PALÁCIO DA PENA

"I just love to play with images!"
Christelle Boulé
Graphic Design Student @ Montréal, Canada

"Seeing is believing."
Dani Eveleigh & Lydia Cock-burnsmith
University Students @ Brighton, UK

"Does it bug you?"
Jim Chambers
Art Director @ London, UK

"Ya Baha'u'l-Abha!"
George W. Hatcher
Aerospace Engineer @ Merritt Island, USA

"LOL"
Alexandra Roucheray
Graphic Design Student @ Strasbourg, France

"The best ideas come as jokes. Make your thinking as funny as possible" - by David M. Ogilvy
Hans Keding Becker-Christensen & Louise Ryberg
Design Students @ Copenhagen, Denmark

"Have a conversation with a 3-year-old."
Gabriel Leung
Artist & Photographer @ Hong Kong, China

Autobahn
Graphic Designer @ Utrecht, the Netherlands

"Sex, drugs, money & murder."
Dipesh Pandya, Freelance Creative Director & Graphic Designer @ Paris, France

"Honda!"
Geoffroy de Boismenu, Photographer @ Paris, France

"Sometimes when you fall, you fly. Fair dinkum."
Garry Trinh
Artist @ Sydney, Australia

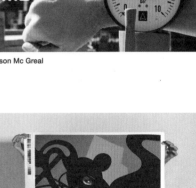

Allison Mc Greal

"It may seem morbid, but I like being reminded of the brevity of life, it actually gives me more incentive to enjoy each day to the fullest."
Noah Scalin
Creative Director & Founder of Another Limited Rebellion @ Richmond (Virginia), USA

"Love & laugh."
misu2020 / Laura Weider
Character Artist @ Berlin, Germany

Tomi Vollauschek
Co-founder & Director of FL@33 Ltd. @ Frankfurt, Germany

"Be kind, embrace your desires and don't be shy!"
Jasper Goodall
Illustrator & Designer @ Brighton, UK

"I'm young and I need the money."
Kasper Strömman
Illustration @ Helsinki, Finland

Agathe Jacquillat
Co-founder & Director of FL@33 Ltd. @ Paris, France

"Functionalism."
pleaseletmedesign
Graphic Designer @ Brussels, Belgium

"Weird stuff is fun!"
Leo Lei
Graphic Designer @ Hong Kong, China

Noelle Lamonica
Tattoo Artist @ Buffalo (New York), USA

"Fun everywhere!!!!!!!"
Sonya Suhariyan
Artist & Illustrator @ Rostov-on-Don, Russia

"Art for art's sake."
Crispin Finn
Designer & Artist @ London, UK

"Better done than perfect."
Joshua Callaghan
Artist @ Los Angeles, USA

"Life must move on."
Ho Yan Yee
Editorial Assistant @ Hong Kong, China

"It may seem morbid, but I like being reminded of the brevity of life, it actually gives me more incentive to enjoy each day to the fullest."
Noah Scalin
Creative Director & Founder of Another Limited Rebellion @ Richmond (Virginia), USA

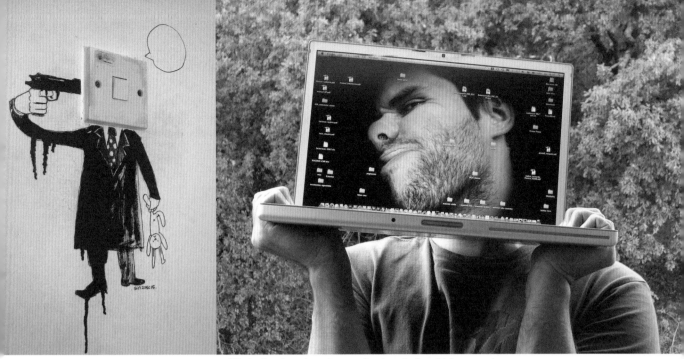

Yee Sin
Designer @ Kuala Lumpur, Malaysia

"Having fun, depends much more of us than of others. It's important that we seek for ways of having fun. But sometimes that quest simply goes wrong!"
Nuno Martins
Designer @ Oporto, Portugal

"Punker than you."
TJ Harmon
Graphic Designer @ Carlsbad (California), USA

"Getting up in the morning, catching the bus, sitting in the park (should be the celebration of a mystery), coming home, getting drunk (wasted), falling asleep (dreaming)."
Bruno Caracol, Pizza Delivery @ Lisbon, Portugal

Gudrun Lilja Gunnlaugsdottir

"Getting up in the morning, catching the bus, sitting in the park (should be the celebration of a mystery), coming home, getting drunk (wasted), falling asleep (dreaming)."
Bruno Caracol, Pizza Delivery @ Lisbon, Portugal

"Do what you like best and keep on playing!"
Florentijn Hofman
Artist @ Rotterdam, the Netherlands

Audoin Desforges
Paris, France

"Weird stuff is fun!"
Leo Lei
Graphic Designer @ Hong Kong, China

"My life is like a real-life 'Funhouse' minus the Pat Sharpe hairdo."
Lauren Davies
Life Size Illustrator @ London, UK

"I'm young and I need the money."
Kasper Strömman
Illustration @ Helsinki, Finland

"Work with what surrounds you, get the hidden qualities out of it and emphasize them!"
Paul Swagerman & Rutger Vos
Graphic & Interactive Designers @ Rotterdam, the Netherlands

"Fun-Playing is to take the real in order to expand it into a created, fictive situation that generates another perception of the reality that appeals to the memories or knowledge of the espectators."
Martí Guixe, Designer @ Barcelona, Spain, Berlin, Germany

"Getting up in the morning, catching the bus, sitting in the park (should be the celebration of a mystery), coming home, getting drunk (wasted), falling asleep (dreaming)."
Bruno Caracol, Pizza Delivery @ Lisbon, Portugal

"Sex, drugs, money & murder."
Dipesh Pandya, Freelance Creative Director & Graphic Designer @ Paris, France

"Honda!"
Geoffroy de Boismenu, Photographer @ Paris, France

"Punker than you."
TJ Harmon
Graphic Designer @ Carlsbad (California), USA

"In which form does the network data world manifest itself in our everyday life? What comes back from cyberspace into physical space? How do digital innovations influence our everyday actions?"
Aram Bartholl, Artist @ Berlin, Germany

"Rhythm is it!"
Michael Seibert
Graphic Design Student @ Berlin, Germany

"It may seem morbid, but I like being reminded of the brevity of life, it actually gives me more incentive to enjoy each day to the fullest."
Noah Scalin, Creative Director & Founder of Another Limited Rebellion @ Richmond (Virginia), USA

Allison Mc Greal

"Sometimes when you fall, you fly. Fair dinkum."
Garry Trinh
Artist @ Sydney, Australia

"Please pass the Bauhaus."
Steve Rura & Tiziana Haug
Art Directors & Graphic Designers @ New York City, USA

"Discover beauty in spontaneity."
Debra Anderson
CEO & Founder of Culture Shock Marketing LLC @ New York City, USA

"In which form does the network data world manifest itself in our everyday life?"
Andre Wiesmayr
Artist @ Berlin, Germany

"Work hard be nice."
Deanne Cheuk
Art Director @ New York City, USA

"Fresh thoughts and perceptions can change the way people think."
Andrea Lorca
Photographer, Art Director & Designer @ São Paulo, Brazil

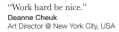

"Almost every problem in life is a playground for a creative solution!"
Moe Minkara
Creative Director @ Zagreb, Croatia

"Strength & Honour. Unleash Hell!"
Bruno Sellés
Creative Director & Founder of Vasava @ Barcelona, Spain

"If we have a good time making a visual (without forgetting the strictness), we are probably sure the visual will be a good one."
Akatre, Graphic Design Studio @ Saint Ouen, France

"Lectures."
Matteo Mastronardi
Art Director @ Paris, France

"P play L play A play Y play"
Melle Hammer
Graphic Designer, Typographer & Artist @ Amsterdam, the Netherlands

"Accidents and sagacity of things which were not in quest of."
Anna Fidalgo
Graphic Designer @ London, UK

"Not all those who wander are lost."
Annabel Vere
Photographer @ London, UK

"In the kingdom of the blind, the three-eyed is me."
Joe A. Scerri
Graphic Designer @ Zürich, Switzerland

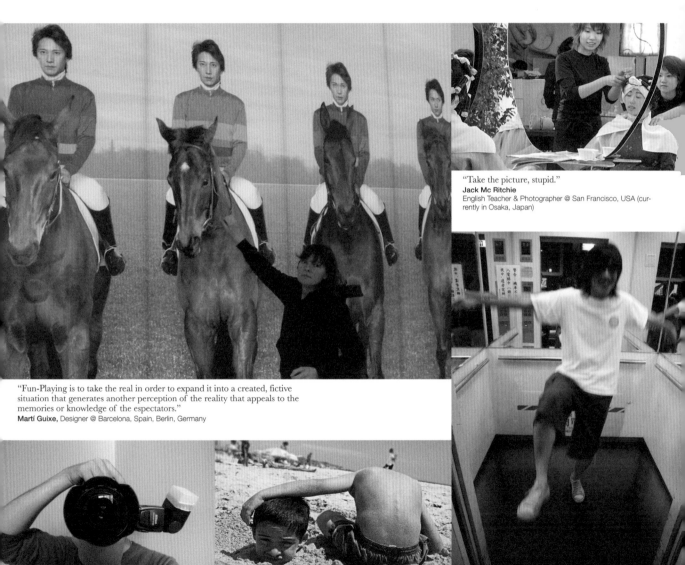

"Take the picture, stupid."
Jack Mc Ritchie
English Teacher & Photographer @ San Francisco, USA (currently in Osaka, Japan)

"Fun-Playing is to take the real in order to expand it into a created, fictive situation that generates another perception of the reality that appeals to the memories or knowledge of the espectators."
Martí Guixe, Designer @ Barcelona, Spain, Berlin, Germany

"You're reality is my fiction."
Erik Erdokozi
Web & Graphic Designer & Photographer @ Timisoara, Romania

"Hi mom - I'm on TV in a book!"
Gui Seiz
Art Director @ London, UK

"Make everyone happy."
Even Wu
Designer @ Taipei, Taiwan

Maija Louekari
Designer & Illustrator @ Helsinki, Finland

"Believe in the process. Be authentic. Be brave. Do it with passion and after all have fun."
Clemens Bladermann
Designer @ Munich, Germany

"Work hard be nice."
Deanne Cheuk
Art Director @ New York City, USA

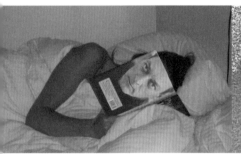

Vanessa van Dam & Diederik Martens
Graphic Designer, Founder of Twones @ Amsterdam, the Netherlands

"Start hunting for surprises!"
Basiaan de Wolff
Crossmedia Storyteller @ Amsterdam, the Netherlands

"In order to be irreplaceable one must always be different."
- by Gabrielle Bonheur "Coco" Chanel
Claudia C. Sandor
Graphic Designer @ Oslo, Norway

"I like to use different kinds of raw materials and play with volumes and formats to mislead the spectator."
Sarah Kahn
Graphic Designer & Art Director @ Paris, France

"Humour, or entertainment is a good way to get people look at your work, just like elegance, or style, something that makes people look, that makes you curious."
Martin Fengel @ Munich, Germany

"Accidents and sagacity of things which were not in quest of."
Anna Fidalgo
Graphic Designer @ London, UK

"Let's foomp! and foomp means doing something crazy."
Mieke Driessen (a.k.a. Foomp)
Artist & Character Designer @ Berlin, Germany

"Laugh often, and well?"
Juliette Cezzar
Graphic Designer @ New York City, USA

"All I want is to be happy, and I think design and creation can do that. I try to see things from a different aspect. You can find happiness everywhere, but you just have to work at seeing it."
Maxime Archambault, Freelance Fashion & Graphic Designer @ Montreal, Canada

"Brainstorming."
Matteo Mastronardi & Vincent Burgeon
Art Directors @ Paris, France

"You can't bolt the door with a boiled carrot."
Stephen Hackett
Film Maker @ Belfast, Ireland

"Ya Baha'u'l-Abha!"
George W. Hatcher
Aerospace Engineer @ Merritt Island, USA

"Her smile is contagious."
Kfdid
Postgraduate @ Hong Kong, China

"Ahoy, and other nautical expressions!"
Lainey Hope
Graphic Designer @ Leeds, UK

P.230
DESIGNERS'
PROFILE

GET TO
KNOW THE
CRAFTS-
MEN

ADEARFRIEND™

Chris Ro is a graphic designer currently based in New York. He holds an undergraduate degree in Architecture from UC Berkeley, and also a MFA in Graphic Design from the Rhode Island School of Design. He is a member of the AIGA and is a full-time contributor to the graphic design journal, Graphic Hug.

Ro loves graphic design and very much delights in all that can be classified as extremely complex yet ultimately, very simple. He enjoys the occasional blending of two dimensions with three dimensions, and the dialogue that takes place between the two.

P. 66-67

ADRIAN NEWELL

After graduated with First Class Honours from the University of Salford in 2007, Adrian Newell is now working for a design agency in London, UK.

P. 72-73

AESTHETICALLY LOYAL

Anthony Kolber is a graphic designer from Melbourne, Australia. Graduated from Swinburne University in 2006, with a degree with honours in design, Kolber's design approach is greatly influenced by the ideologies of Bob Gill, Alan Fletcher and conceptual artists such as Joseph Kosuth and Hans Haacke.

P. 137

ALAN WOO

Alan Woo is a graphic designer who recently graduated from the Emily Carr Institute in Vancouver, Canada. He is interested in working in various mediums that can function together to bridge unusual dichotomies and draw from one another.

P. 136

ALEX OSTROWSKI

Alex Ostrowski is an independent graphic designer and art director working in London, England. He enjoys his discipline's responsibility to 'get through to people' and tries to inject as much fun and energy into his work as possible. He also loves working with other creative people including frequent illustrative collaborator Hattie Newman.

P. 21

ALEX WOOLLEY

Graduated from Kingston University in 2007, Alex Woolley is now living and working in London.

P. 154-155

P.230
DESIGNERS'
PROFILE

GET TO
KNOW THE

ATELIER BOW-WOW

Atelier Bow-Wow is a Tokyo-based firm founded by Yoshiharu Tsukamoto and Momoyo Kaijima in 1992. With interests ranging from urban research to architectural design and public artwork, the duo has designed over 20 detached houses such as 'Gae House' and 'House & Atelier Bow-Wow.' Their recent projects such as 'Hanamidori Cultural Centre' has marked an expansion towards projects in a larger scale. Their experimental projects with micro-public-space have been exhibited across the world such as Korea, China, Japan, Italy and Brazil.

P. 174-175

ATYPYK

ATYPK sounds Greek, but it is actually from France. The friendly business enjoys making completely unnecessary things. ATYPYK is honest with what they do and never steal ideas. They promise a lot, but they also understand that they can't guarantee anything. There is no specific job set for members at ATYPYK where everybody does everything in the office.

P. 113, 144-145, 147

AVRIL LORETI

Avril Loreti designs modern home decor and accessories that add extra creative thoughts and design sensibility to people's life. Described as simple, minimal, innovative and pretty, Loreti's designs stem from her interest in objects and ideas that make up daily life. Loreti is attracted to everything from permanent icons and structures that set the stage for modern life, to the fleeting pieces of paper and ephemera that are here today and gone tomorrow. Their presence and patterns are what influence her work.

P. 34-35

AXEL PEEMÖLLER DESIGN

Axel Peemöller studied graphic design in Düsseldorf and Hamburg, Germany and Melbourne, Australia where he did a master by research, and he works as a freelance art director/designer for design studios and clients around the globe.

Peemöller loves design, architecture, art, loud music, animals (especially his dog named Bones), the outdoors, oceans and mountains, surfing and snowboarding. He spends a lot of time in foreign places and is currently living in Hamburg, Germany.

P. 152-153

AZE DESIGN

AZE design is a design studio established in 2006 by Anna Kotowicz (born in 1978) and Artur Puszkarewicz (born in 1976). Their partnership started in 2004 at Warsaw Nizio Design International for the Warsaw Uprising Museum project – the first multimedia museum exhibition in Poland.

Their education in architecture, applied graphics and art history was the starting point to create objects that reflect marriage between those disciplines. They transform everyday situations into objects mostly based on their observations in daily life.

P. 108-109

AZUMI AND DAVID (A'N'D)

Azumi and David both studied fashion at Central Saint Martins, London but met in The Troubadour Coffee House in London's Earl's Court in May 1995. The couple has progressed through a variety of creative projects - initially with limited edition artist's books and performance art, moving gradually on to fashion and accessory associated 'things to wear.'

Azumi and David presented their first fashion accessories, 'piercing' and 'ear wax' - foam and wax earplug earrings, branded A'N'D, to The Pineal Eye, London in April 1999 followed by Colette, Paris in September 1999. Their new collections of 'things to wear' are shown in a Paris showroom twice a year ever since 2003 and are available in over 40 stores in major cities such as London, Paris, New York, Tokyo and Milan.

P. 26-27, 124-129

BERBER SOEPBOER, MICHIEL SCHUURMAN

Born in Schiermonnikoog in 1983, Berber Soepboer graduated in 2007 from the fashion department at Gerrit Rietveld Academie. She is specialised in designing clothes that can be worn in different ways, allowing wearers the freedom to wear the cloth to their liking.

Born Amsterdam in 1974, Michiel Schuurman studied graphic design and typography for two years at Koninklijke Academie voor de Beeldende Kunsten Den Haag and graduated in graphic design from Gerrit Rietveld Academy Amsterdam in 2002. He is specialised in typography. He designs his own typefaces and likes working with black and white.

P. 122-123

BOYS DON'T CRY

Boys Don't Cry addresses the possibilities of form where new methods can be developed to fulfill the promises of popular culture, marketing and communication. They do that in a converging creative situation through numerous collaborations and agency networks.

Boys Don't Cry identifies the stories that both the studio and their customers would like to be a part of, stories that are welcome and inspirational in users' minds. They find the design of most commercial environment has been conceptually left behind and more attention should be given to that.

Boys Don't Cry aims at creating spaces that are worth understanding and investing, and makes such spaces a tool to meet communicative needs between customers and concepts.

P. 196-197

BREANNE TRAMMELL

Breanne Trammell is a multidisciplinary artist living and working in New York City. Her work celebrates normative experiences via 1980s-1990s popular culture, domesticity, cute, kitsch and the culture of collecting, and shares triumphant moments of youth and adulthood which occasionally reveals the dark and embarrassing ones too.

P. 180-183

CHRIS DOROSZ

Chris Dorosz was born in Ottawa in 1972 and graduated with a BFA from Concordia University in Montreal, as well as a MFA from the Nova Scotia College of Art and Design in Halifax, Canada. In 2003, he won the Royal Bank of Canada's New Painting Competition and was then represented in various public and private collections in Canada, the US and Europe. His studio practice is based in San Francisco.

P. 202-205

COCHAE

Founded in 2003, cochae creates with a theme of 'playing design,' with production ranging from graphic origami and paper puzzles, to origami workshops at art museums and toys from a new point of view. The unit, led by Yosuke Jikuhara and Miki Takeda, aims to create things that everyone enjoys and that for amateurs in a good sense. 'cochae' means 'welcome first-timers.'

P. 52

DOMINIC WILCOX

Born in Sunderland, Dominic Wilcox is an artist, designer and everything in between. His work is usually based around everyday objects and human behaviour. His time is split between working on his own personal projects and his comissioned work. Recent commissions include Nike where Dominic ended up superglueing 15000 plastic football figures together into various shapes and a charity auction event for bin company Vipp where he turned an ordinary bin into an automatically playing xylophone.

P. 114-115

DRAFT CO., LTD

Draft Co., Ltd was derived from Satory Miyata Design Office, founded by Satoru Miyata in 1978 upon his departure from Nippon Design Center. Draft's clients include Jack Daniel's, The Yokohama Rubber co ltd. (PRGR), Mos Food Services Inc., Lacoste, Japan Energy Corporation, Wacoal Corp, etc. The award-winning company is also known for its D-BROS product line launched in 1995.

P. 10-11, 17, 22-23, 38-41, 50-51, 56-57, 59, 94-95, 118-121

EMMA HACK

Through dedication and passion for craft, Emma Hack's 20 years of career has evolved from being a children's face painter, qualified hairdresser and make-up artist, to an acclaimed artist. Her Wallpaper 2005, 2007 and 2008 collections feature a series of Florence Broadhurst wallpaper designs mixed with her body illustration. Hack enjoys working with the late Australian designer's aesthetically pleasing designs due to the lovely energy and character combined with human form.

P. 176-179

EMMA SMART

Emma Smart is a quiet lass from the north west of England who works as a graphic designer by day and a crafter by night. Her witty, thought-provoking design style allows her to create work that makes people smile, evidenced by the range of lunchboxes she created for a student brief while studying at Loughborough University. Smart's craftier side is kept busy recycling old jumpers into making plushies, screen printing cushions and experimenting with textiles.

P. 36-37

FACE

FACE is an expansion of conventional accessories and methods of facial adornment with concepts drawn on the paradoxes of function, pseudo-functions, wearability and absurdity. David Toro and Solomon Chase reference the diverse traditions in jewellry, adornment and non-verbal communication, using particular materials and shapes to connote meanings and references.

Toro specialises in photography and sculpture, and also the convergence of the two. Chase has been working in the axis of fashion and art with diverse media as well as consulting on footwear and accessory design.

P. 68-71

FACE37

Face37 is founded by Rick Banks, who was born in Manchester in 1985 and brought up in the nearby town, Bolton. After graduating from University in 2007 with a degree in graphic design, Banks moved to London where he now lives and works.

P. 84-87

P.233
DESIGNER
PROFILE

GET TO
KNOW TH
CRAFTS-
MEN

FELIX LOBELIUS

Currently based in Sydney, Swedish-born Felix Lobelius has been suffering from the incurable disease of graphic design since the hectic second year at Billy Blue College of Design. He finds inspiration in old heroes such as Josef Müller Brockmann and Wim Crouwel, as well as modern graphic leaders such as MadeThought, Frost, Spin and SEA. After graduating in December 2008, Felix has since worked as a designer at Surry Hills based design agency There.

P. 12-13

FINN MAGEE

Finn Magee graduated with a BA in Industrial Design from the National College of Art and Design, Ireland in 2004, where his following MA in Design Products at the Royal College of Art in London fostered his interest in advertising and the construction of meaning through image.

Magee's RCA show investigated the potential of advertising techniques in product design, in particular looking at how mechanism such as juxtaposition, humour and surprise can function in products as opposed to adverts. Magee's Flat Life Lights are currently in development with Artemide, an Italian lighting company. He has exhibitions at Design Mai in Berlin, the Salon di Mobil, Milan and the Design Museum in London.

P. 88-89

GRAPHIC DESIGN STUDIO BY YURKO GUTSULYAK

Ukrainian-born Yurko Gutsulyak graduated in marketing and management from Technological University of Podillia in 2000 and worked as a marketing specialist since. Gutsulyak moved to Kyiv and start his dream career as a designer in 2001. He started his own business - Graphic design studio by Yurko Gutsulyak in 2005.

Despite having received no formal art education, Gutsulyak has gained solid experience in real life projects and Throughout the years, he has won over 30 national and international awards.

P. 16, 82-83

Hh

HÉCTOR SERRANO STUDIO

Founded by Héctor Serrano in London in 2000, Héctor Serrano Studio's activities are divided into product, space, communication and laboratory work. Their projects combine innovation with the communication of familiar ideas in unusual and inventive ways, and their products have been exhibited extensively in museums such as the V&A, London and Cooper-Hewitt, National Design Museum, New York and become part of the different collections of the Central Museum of Amsterdam. The office has received different awards such as the Peugeot Design Award and the Premio Nacional de Diseño No Aburridos. Their clients include Roca, Moooi, ICEX Spanish Ministry of Industry, Tourism and Trade, Droog Design, Metalarte, La Casa Encendida (Caja Madrid) and Valencia City Council among others.

P. 48-49

HELMO

Helmo is the graphic design duo Thomas Couderc and Clement Vauchez, who create posters, books, museography, pictures and even architectural designs. They established 'la bonne merveille' with Thomas Dimetto in 2002, which remains today the name of the workspace they share in Montreuil, Paris. They decided to change the composition in 2007. While the design duo established the graphic design studio 'Helmo,' Dimetto started to work with Marcel, a French advertising agency.

P. 184-187

HENRY HADLOW

Graphic designer Henry Hadlow is an evangelical atheist and loves schadenfreude. He was once a scientist researching cancer-drugs but he is happier working as a designer, cultivating eccentricities and working at night. Having lived in Bath, Berlin and Hong Kong, Hadlow is now based in London and thinking if there's somewhere else he should live and experience. He rides everywhere with his racing bike and eats lovely dark chocolates every day.

P. 158-159

Ii

IGOR EŠKINJA (ADN GALERÍA)

Represented by ADN Galería, Igor Eškinja was born in Rijeka, Croatia, in 1975 and studied Fine Arts in Venice, Italy, until graduation in 2002. He tries to create situations at the same time worrying and amazing, critical and subversive, realising little and simple interventions in the exhibiting space, stretching out to minimalism concerning the choice of materials and the expressivity. Eškinja's works are declaration of falseness of the vision, of relativity of reference systems, in a complete revolution of our experience.

P. 138-139

Jj

JAMIE WIECK

Jamie Wieck is a London-based graphic designer and illustrator who enjoys solving problems.

P. 58

JAN VORMANN

Jan Vormann was born in Bamberg, Germany in 1983, and is based in St. Petersburg since 2007. Vormann studied Art History and Restauration at Otto-Friedrich-Universität, Bamberg before he pursued Fine Arts studies at Kunst-Hochschule Berlin-Weißensee, Germany in 2004. He was awarded the DAAD Stipendium at Muchina Hochschule für Angewandte Kunst, St. Petersburg in 2008.

Vormann had his solo exhibition 'Cirles and Spheres' in 2008. His works have also been exhibited in various places, ranging from galleries in Germany, Denmark, Iran and Russia.

P. 134-135

JEAN-YVES LEMOIGNE

Jean-Yves Lemoigne is an advertising photographer with a focus on magic in everyday life. In his surrealistic vision, daily routine falls in another dimension. He loves to shoot smart and surprising photos that do not look like classic advertising. He has been working with magazines like Amusement, WAD, Technikart and Le Monde.

P. 162-165

JESSE KIRSCH

Graphic designer Jesse Kirsch has a passion for typography, minimalism, packaging and three-dimensional creations. After honing his skills at New York's School of Visual Arts, Kirsch went on to design, for clients including Atlantic Records and Columbia University. He currently lives and works at home in Edison, New Jersey.

P. 18-19

JINGREN ART DESIGN STUDIO

Award-winning book designer and illustrator Lu Jingren was born in Shanghai, China, in 1947. He had been a member of the editorial committee and senior art editor when worked in China Youth Publishing House. During the 1990s, he studied under the guidance of the visual art designer, Prof. Sugiura Kohei of College of Art Engineering in Kobe, Japan. He serves at Tsinghua University as a Professor in the Academy of Arts and Design, Guest Professor in the Central Academy of Fine Arts, and an AGI member since 2006.

Lu started Jingren Art Design Studio in 1998. His work strives for a balance between intellectualism, tradition and modern visual expressions so as to establish an oriental style without drawing directly from the past and a modern spirit without referencing western culture.

P. 54-55

JOON & JUNE

Joon & June is a project group composed of Kim Joonhyun and Kwon Minjoo. Joonhyun Kim was born in 1983 and he studied at Konkuk University, Seoul. Kim had been in several exhibitions, such as the Tokyo TETSUSON Exhibition, Seoul Living Design Fair Exhibition and 100% Design Tokyo Exhibition in 2008. He had won a bronze prize at MUJI AWARD 03 with 'A Precise Stapler.'

P. 102

JULIE KRAKOWSKI

After her education in Visual Arts, Julie Krakowski moved on to study textile design at La Cambre National School of Visual Art, Brussels. Julie's work and design processes cross multiple artistic fields and techniques.

P. 30-31

Kk

K.K. NORMAL

K.K. Normal was established in 2000 to manage Ross McBride's product, furniture, and interior projects. McBride was born in the Northeastern United States in 1962 and earned his bachelor's degree in graphic design from the California Institute of the Arts. Upon graduation in 1985, McBride moved promptly to Tokyo where he has lived ever since, and furthered his graphic design studies as a research student at Nihon Daigaku (Japan University).

McBride worked in several design offices, including Igarashi Studio under the auspices of Takenobu Igarashi before he went independent in 1991. In 1997 McBride initiated a move to pursue his interests in product and furniture design with his first public exhibition '12 Timepieces' at the Ozone Gallery in Shinjuku, Tokyo. He has worked on projects for Duende, E&Y, Maxray, Starbucks Japan, etc.

P. 28-29

KEITH HANCOX

Keith Hancox is a 21-year-old graphic designer who has recently graduated from Bath Spa University in the UK. He works across various media ranging from editorial design, posters and typefaces to identities and website design. He is interested in sustainability and interactivity within design and also enjoys cross-disciplinary collaboration.

P. 130-131

KUMI YAMASHITA

Kumi Yamashita was born in Japan and is now based in Queens, New York.

P. 198-201

KYOUEI DESIGN

Kouichi Okamoto was born in Shizuoka City, Japan, in 1970. He made his debut in 1997 with 'BEKKOU-Hi Lite' released on X-trax(NL), followed by his first solo record in two years' time. In 2006, he established his own design office, Kyouei design and introduce his work with exhibition 'Two Days & Four Products' at Shizuoka Prefectural Museum of Art. He also actively participates in design events including ICFF(NY), 100% Design Tokyo, St. Etienne 5th biennial International Design Festival, and recently the 'kansei-Japan Design Exhibition' in Paris, produced and curated by Hexa project.

P. 90-91, 103, 146

MALIN HOLMSTRÖM

Malin Holmström is a graphic designer who has mostly been working on identity, packaging, and print projects. Malin was born in a small town in Sweden in 1985 and has moved to Australia in 2005 to study communication design. She received her bachelor's degree in December 2008.

P. 64-65

MASH

Since its establishment in 2002 Adelaide, Australia by Dom Roberts and James Brown, Mash has been working in many facets of branding, design, visual identity, web design, photography, art direction and copywriting. They creates truly memorable work without the ridiculous theories and processes, and caters specially to clients who truly want to build their brand with creativity and originality.

Mash thrives on collaborating with like-minded creative individuals and bodies to construct, present and represent all that is visual. By developing a circle of hotographers, copy writers, illustrators and stylists, the agency is capable of handling a variety of projects with specific teams.

P. 112

MELVIN GALAPON

Illustrator and designer Melvin Galapon was born in the South of England in 1981, yet hails from Burnley, a small town in the Northwest of England. Despite his recent graduation from Central St. Martin, he has already managed to build an impressive client list comprising Wallpaper*, The New York Times, The Guardian and Howies to name a few. Galapon is currently based in London where he works on a mix of illustrations, installations and design work.

P. 20

MERCI BERNARD

Passionate and open-minded, young and polyvalent French graphic designer Merci Bernard explores all visual fields with the view of creating astonishing pictures. Bernard received eduation in École Supérieure d'Arts Appliqués de Bourgogne (ESAAB), and is currently a member of the French graphic collective Think Experimental.

P. 60-61

MIKE AND MAAIKE INC.

Mike and Maaike create experimental designs and unexpected solutions for products, furniture, wearables and environments. Maaike Evers is a Dutch while Mike Simonian is a Californian. Their distinct backgrounds and experimental approach to design create strong conceptual foundations that often result in the unexpected.

P. 42-43

MUSIC FOR PATTERNS

Music for Patterns is Melissa Duarte and Pipa. Their work is rooted on the Latin American legacies of geometric abstraction and experimentalism, employing current technologies to further these lines of research. Like avant-garde artists such as Julio Le Parc, Carlos Cruz-Diez and Hélio Oiticica, MFP invests geometry with life, expanding it into space and inviting viewers to have a highly sensory experience.

P. 210-213

NENDO

Tokyo-based design firm nendo is founded in 2002 with Oki Sato (b. Canada, 1977, M. Arch. Waseda University) as its principal. The firm realises its goal of bringing small surprises to people through multidisciplinary practice in areas including architecture, interiors, furniture, industrial products and graphic design.

P. 32-33, 192-195

NIKOLAUS SCHMIDT GRAPHIC DESIGN & TYPOGRAPHY

Nikolaus Schmidt studied advertising and marketing at the Advertising Academy of the Vienna Economics Institute from 1999 to 2001 and gained a degree with honours in graphic and media design/experimental typography at the London College of Communication in 2004.

Schmidt worked as a freelance graphic designer in Vienna, Austria upon graduation and later served at European Society of Radiology as the head of internal graphic department. Schmidt founded 'Represent studio' for visual communication design practices in 2007.

P. 100-101

NINA MRSNIK

Nina Mrsnik was born in 1982 in Ljubljana, Slovenija, and has moved to Treviso, Italy, and studied product design at IUAV Architectural University of Venice after high school. She did an internship in Fabrica, Italy, in Benetton's research center where she worked in the product design department.
Nina did an exchange in Portugal where she studied product design at the Communication and Art faculty of Aveiro, and is currently doing an MA in product design at the Royal college of Art. She aims to do product design as an illustrator.

P. 156-157

NOTO FUSAI

Noto-Fusai is a designer duo consisting of designers Noto Hirotsugu and Noto Miyo, who launched the alternative t-shirt brand [SHIKISAI] in 2005 to explore the alternative possibilities of t-shirt design, incorporating the interactivity, the mundanity, and the sense of fun, through the use of black print on white surface.

P. 110-111, 116

OHYESCOOLGREAT.

Ohyescoolgreat. is a co-operation for design and production of print, web and public spaces with focuses on social awareness. They work internationally but are based in the Netherlands.

P. 140-141

PERSIJN BROERSEN & MARGIT LUKÁCS

Persijn Broersen and Margit Lukács are the artist duo based in Amsterdam, the Netherlands. Their practice ranges from video installations, drawings, murals and films to online columns and video clips.

The returning theme in their work is how the individual relates to the ever growing outside world, which often translates into structures with an initial sense of order that degenerates into chaos and falls apart. Utopic and dystopic fantasy landscapes operate in a number of ways in Broersen and Lukács's work, showing how various narratives presented by the mass media and general culture come to constitute whole worlds for the people who absorb them.

P. 206-209

PETTER HANBERGER

Petter Hanberger studys graphic design and advertising at Beckmans College of Design in Stockholm, Sweden.

P. 115

PIA KNIGHT

From print design for pimps to art direction for dandruff commercials, Pia's career has been a varied one to say the least. Living in Italy and working at Fabrica, she grew creatively and literally due to a new found love of deep fried mozzarella. She's now a meat-eating vegetarian who lives a happy life in the heart of east London. Pia has lost her fish phobia and sold her soul to the devil. By some she is still known as 'nipple girl'. But her new boss doesn't know that.

P. 46-47

POLAR

Barcelona-based Polar likes taking each project as a unique process. They produce a variety of projects including publishing, exhibition and event identity, signage, corporate identity and anything that interests them. On certain occasion the studio collaborats with other designers, architects, writers, illustrators, photographers, web programmers and anybody whom shares the ideals of the creative process of the project.

P. 104-107

RITA

Rita's world is both two-dimensional and three-dimensional. Rita believes that graphic, object and event design are naturally interconnected. Working together, these modes of design complement each other, inspiring new creative solutions in form, function and communication. Inherent in Rita's style is the combination of different aspects of design. In each project, the graphic treatment is integral to the format, and vice versa.

P. 148-151

RUNE MORTENSEN DESIGN STUDIO

Born and raised in Flekkefjord, a small town in the south of Norway, Rune Mortensen moved to Oslo after high school and learnt to become an art director. After graduating he spent two years working for Norwegian pioneer designer Egil Haraldsen, doing mainly book sleeves and film posters, and later at DDB Oslo while designing sleeves and posters for friends at the same time. He started his own studio in 2000 to focus on music and publishing.

P. 166-169

SARAH NAPIER

Sarah Kahn is a French graphic designer and art director based in Paris. She graduated from Esag Penninghen, Paris, in 2008 with her final year project 'Les Toiles Humaines' which developed her emotional intellect with some computing tools and functions. She's now a freelance art director for a few fashion and cultural magazine.

P. 44-45

SLINKACHU

Slinkachu started his street art installation and photography project 'Little People' in 2006. 'Little People' involves the remodelling and painting of miniature model train set characters. The street-based side of Slinkachu's work plays with the notion of surprise, encouraging city-dwellers to be more aware of their surroundings. The scenes he sets up, more evident through the photography, and the titles he gave these scenes aim to reflect the loneliness and melancholy of living in a big city, almost being lost and overwhelmed. But underneath this, there is always some humour. He wants people to be able to empathise with the tiny people in his works.

P. 160-161

STUDIO-SM

Studio-SM is a small design studio based in the lovely Stoke Newington in east London. It has been in operation since 2007, and is currently run by Sofia and Magnus.

P. 142-143

SURREALIEN

Surrealien is a studio and creative think tank founded by Tom Hanke. The uncommon fields of knowledge which Hanke touched – philosophy, art history, product design and the self-taugh electrical engineering – are reflected in the studio's broad field of interest. They works on the edge of design, art, technology and social sciences. Recent projects include interactive installations for exhibitions, interior-, stage- and set designs, not to mention educational concepts.

P. 172-173, 188-191

THE CHASE

Over the last two decades, The Chase has gained their reputation as one of the leading graphic design and branding agencies in Britain. Led by the founding partners Ben Casey and Lionel Hatch, The Chase has always had a simple and consistent approach to delivering clever and tailored communication solutions. The studio has won over 300 awards for creativity, innovation and effectiveness, which put them consistently at the top four design agencies of Britain.

P. 53, 92-93

THE MAP OFFICE

The Map Office, LLC is a nine-person graphic design atelier based in New York and Boston that has extensive experience in print, brand and environmental design. Manoeuvring between print, motion graphics, web, information architecture and environmental design, they 'weave visual design and technology with architecture to create compelling experiences.' Their recent clients include UCLA Department of Architecture and Urban Design, The Kitchen, Sophie, Taxter and Spengemann, Della Valle and Bernheimer, The Studio Museum in Harlem, Jazz at Lincoln Center, JET, Harry. N Abrams, Lane Crawford, etc.

P. 214-216

TOBY NG

Toby Ng was a graphic design graduate from Central St. Martins in 2008. He is now looking for work opportunities in the creative field in London. His work has been featured in some design blogs and magazines. Ng is also very into photography and he has got into the Taylor Wessing Photographic Portrait Prize. Ng's work has been exhibited in the National Portrait Gallery in London till February 2009.

P. 14-15

US DESIGN STUDIO

us is a London-based design studio who believes design should stem from good ideas no matter how big or small. us creates work that excites, inspires and most importantly answers the brief. Their work is not a style that people buy into – it's rather a service that they provide to meet clients' needs.

P. 96-97, 132-133

VANESSA VAN DAM

Vanessa van Dam's work is based on a four-pronged approach to design consisting of developing a concept, the use of literal naming of objects, layering of meaning and establishing a level of activity with the viewer. The use of this complex matrix results in work that can be humorous and is always greater than the sum of its parts. It always has 'clearness' in it. Van Dam works mostly for the 'cultural world,' such as museums, architects, photographers, artists, (literature) publishers, etc. Besides designing, she teaches graphic design, takes part in juries as well as design commissions.

P. 24-25

VAUGHAN WARD

Vaughan Ward graduated from the University of Brighton in 2007 and is now enjoying his life in London.

P. 78-81

VICTION:WORKSHOP LTD.

Founded by Victor Cheung in 2001, viction:workshop is a multi-disciplinary design house focusing on graphics and creative arts. Its publishing arm viction:ary has developed an international reputation for its distinctively-designed books with cutting-edge content on graphic design, illustration, typography and packaging revealing the emerging trends and talents in the creative scene. Available worldwide through an international network of distributors, viction:ary books have proved to be highly-collectible, sought-after and have frequently been on the bestseller lists in mainstream bookstores.

P. 62-63, 76-77, 98-99

WALKER

Pius Walker entered the world of adverting as a creative trainee in 1988 at Y&R Zurich and later worked abroad in some of the most established creative agencies including Springer & Jacoby and Jung von Matt in Hamburg, Scholz & Friends in Berlin and Leagas Delaney in London.

Walker founded walker Zurich, the world's smallest advertising agency, in 2003. Awarded "Newcomer Agency of the Year" in 2007 and elected "Advertiser of the Year 2008" in Switzerland the next year, today's walker Zurich is responsible for accounts like Fleurop-Interflora, Swiss Air Rescue REGA and Amnesty International. It currently ranks among the top 40 creative agencies worldwide according to The Gunn Report.

P. 170-171

WWW.JANENRANDOALD.BE

Jan W. Hespeel and Randoald Sabbe graduated in the free graphics and graphic design department at Sint-Lucas Ghent. They were very polite to each other but never had a conversation though. They started to teach at Sint-Lucas in 1997 and soon a certain synergy appeared. In 2004 they started their collaboration and recently named their studio 'janenrandoald'.

'janenrandoald' is now one of the most awarded graphic design studios in Belgium. They have a broad range of clients including Antwerpse Musea, STAM, Concertzaal De Bijloke, De Werf Brugge & Véronique Branquinho.

P. 74-75

ACKNOWLEDGEMENT

We would like to thank all the designers and companies who made significant contribution to the compilation of this book. Without them this project would not be able to accomplish. We would also like to thank all the producers for their invaluable assistance throughout this entire proposal. The successful completion also owes a great deal to many professionals in the creative industry who have given us precious insights and comments. We are also very grateful to many other people whose names did not appear on the credits but have made specific input and continuous support the whole time.

FUTURE EDITION

If you would like to contribute to the next edition of Victionary, please email us your details to submit@victionary.com